OWEN FRANK

WHO

SAID

THAT?

TAKE THE QUOTE QUIZ CHALLENGE

WORKMAN PUBLISHING
NEW YORK

Copyright © 2019 by Owen Frank
Illustrations copyright © 2019 by Dan Springer

All rights reserved. No portion of this book may
be reproduced—mechanically, electronically, or
by any other means, including photocopying—
without written permission of the publisher.
Published simultaneously in Canada by
Thomas Allen & Son Limited.

Library of Congress Cataloging-in-Publication
Data is available.

ISBN 978-1-5235-0678-1

Additional Credit: VICTOR/Digital Vision Vectors/
Getty Images (Light Bulb Icon)

Workman books are available at special discounts
when purchased in bulk for premiums and sales
promotions as well as for fund-raising or educational
use. Special editions or book excerpts can also be
created to specification. For details, contact the
Special Sales Director at the address below, or send
an email to specialmarkets@workman.com.

Workman Publishing Co., Inc.
225 Varick Street
New York, NY 10014-4381
workman.com

WORKMAN is a registered trademark of
Workman Publishing Co., Inc.

Printed in Canada

First printing August 2019

10 9 8 7 6 5 4 3 2 1

CONTENTS

"I hate quotation. Tell me what you know."

—RALPH WALDO EMERSON

For as long as people have used words, people have borrowed words. Among all the things someone might borrow, quotations are unique: They can't be used up. Unlike, say, vinyl records or classic cars, there's no limit to how many times you can take a quote for a spin. Although you might begin to annoy your friends.

Why do we quote? For Emerson, who supplied the epigraph above, quoting is just a clever way to get out of saying something new yourself. But it's also true that an existing quote is often the best way of expressing a truth. Can anyone really improve on the saying popularized by Benjamin Franklin, "Time is money"? (Go ahead. Try.)

Quotations are also comforting. Their familiarity reassures us. "How do people go to sleep?" Dorothy Parker once mused. "I might repeat to myself, slowly and soothingly, a list of quotations beautiful from minds profound—if I can remember any of the damn things."

Of course, there's also aesthetic pleasure. Quotes might ring with truth or sizzle with irony—the ancient Greek maxim "Know thyself" versus Oscar Wilde's "Only the shallow know themselves." Sometimes quotes carry unexpected poetry, as in George S. Patton's "A pint of sweat will save a gallon of blood." Other times their clumsiness is endearing, as when George W. Bush intoned: "They misunderestimated me."

But the crucial point about quotations—and one frequently overlooked—is that *someone really said them.* Often it's not just the words themselves that are special, but the speaker. "Happy Birthday, Mr. President," might be a banal sentiment, but not when it is seductively cooed by Marilyn Monroe. And as English actor Kenneth Williams once remarked, quotes "give us a nodding acquaintance with the originator, which is often socially impressive."

Yet here in the authorship department, we humans don't always do so hot. People are more likely to remember a pithy line than who actually said it. So the quote gravitates toward another big name, and, like it or not, that person gets attribution. Thus our old friend Emerson is now widely credited with the saw: "The reward of a thing well done is to have done it." Yet it was Roman philosopher Seneca who originally uttered it. Go figure.

The internet, in typical fashion, has made the problem of misattribution both more tractable and vastly worse. Boundless resources exist to help verify quotes. Yet if we're honest, most people don't give a rip. Memorable lines tumble around on blogs and social media until, say, Taylor Swift winds up being credited for quotes belonging to Adolf Hitler. (Yes, this really happened.)

. . .

The point of this book is simple: For the most part, you just match the quotation with the person quoted. But first, let's be real about the difficulty here.

It's possible that the person reading this right now is about as familiar with quotations as baseball great Joe DiMaggio was as a young man: "I can remember a reporter asking for a quote, and I didn't know what a quote was," DiMaggio recalled. "I thought it was some kind of a soft drink." If this is you, have no fear! Most of the names in this book are quite famous. Educated guesses can get you pretty far. Regardless, the quotes are fun on their own, whether you care about guessing or not.

On the other hand, you may be a certified quote freak. You might take after Winston Churchill—a quote magnet himself—who once said: *"Bartlett's Familiar Quotations is an admirable work, and I studied it intently."* Not only do you know that John Lennon *didn't* come up with "Life is what happens to you while you're busy making other plans," but you know the name of the obscure cartoonist who did. If you salivate at the thought of correctly identifying a maxim of Benjamin Disraeli's, this book is your rare opportunity to feel cool.

But odds are you fall somewhere between novice and freak. You don't sit around all day memorizing passages from *Paradise Lost,* but neither are you baffled by the most famous expressions (think "To be, or not to be"). You are what we might call a "regular person." For you, this book could be challenging at times, but fun throughout. Plus, no one's keeping score—though we've included a three-point difficulty scale to keep things interesting.

On that point, a quick piece of advice: Rather than try for the nine-in-ten we're taught earns you an "A," it'd be better to treat each quote like an at-bat in baseball, where three-in-ten is admirable. As Hall of Famer Ted Williams wrote: "A .300 hitter, that rarest of breeds these days, goes through life with the certainty that he will fail at his job seven out of ten times." Yep, that's the spirit.

. . .

The book is laid out as follows. Seven thematic sections correspond to some of the major stages and preoccupations of life: **Growing Up**; **Love & Marriage**;

Work & Money; **Politics & War**; **Motivation**; **Aging**; and **Wisdom & Miscellany**. There are thirty quotes per category, each with four answer choices listed.

Interspersed between these sections are mini-games to spice things up. **Finish the Quote** asks the reader to do just that—pick the right ending for each one. In **Out of Context**, the reader guesses what was going on when a quote was spoken. In **Reverso!**, the reader is given a name and must choose which of the quotes the speaker actually said—or vice versa. In **The Scuttlebutt**, each quote is *about* someone who remains unnamed; the task is to find out who that someone is. In **–isms**, the reader is given a list of quotes from a speaker renowned for their unique phraseology, such as Mark Twain or Dolly Parton; four are genuine, four incorrect. Finally, **Head-to-Head** presents eight real quotes and two notable figures who might have said them; the goal is to match the quotes correctly.

OK, that's it. Have fun, and remember: It's just a game. Life goes on.

Then again, as author Jorge Luis Borges once said: "Life itself is a quotation."

GROWING UP

"Who can know the
heart of youth but
youth itself?"

—PATTI SMITH

"Hello, babies. Welcome to Earth. It's hot in the summer and cold in the winter.... There's only one rule that I know of, babies—'God damn it, you've got to be kind.'"

 A Kurt Vonnegut

B Dr. Benjamin Spock

C Fred Rogers

D Hippocrates

DID YOU KNOW?

The so-called Golden Rule—treat others as you'd like to be treated—is present in virtually every major belief system. In Taoism, one "is kind to the kind; he is also kind to the unkind." In Christianity: "Do unto others as you would have them do unto you."

ANSWER: A. One of Vonnegut's most celebrated quotations, this monologue comes from his 1965 novel, *God Bless You, Mr. Rosewater*. The main character plans to deliver these words to his neighbor's newborn twins.

"You're born naked and the rest is drag."

A Allen Ginsberg

B RuPaul

C Lady Gaga

D Jean-Paul Sartre

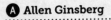

WORD UP

Though it's unclear where and when the word "drag" originated precisely, by the 1870s it was being used in British theater to describe male actors dressed in women's clothing.

ANSWER: B. Perhaps America's most successful drag queen, RuPaul has long eschewed labels. "You can call me he. You can call me she. You can call me Regis and Kathie Lee! I don't care! Just as long as you call me."

"It's only teenage wasteland."

A Patti Smith

B Pete Townshend

C T. S. Eliot

D Jack Kerouac

> **DID YOU KNOW?**
>
> We like to think the youth of every generation are wilder and less innocent than the one before. Yet children born around 2000 are bucking some major trends. Data show they are less likely to drink, smoke, and get pregnant than their predecessors. It's hip to be square!

ANSWER: B. The Who's "Baba O'Riley" was something of an accidental anthem. The song was not a celebration but rather "about the absolute desolation of teenagers at Woodstock," said Townshend.

"An ugly baby is a very nasty object—and the prettiest is frightful when undressed."

A John Updike

B John Waters

C Nancy Astor

D Queen Victoria

SEE ALSO:

"Every newborn baby is a little savage."

—**DARYL GATES,**
chief of the Los Angeles Police Department (1978–1992)

ANSWER: D. Victoria birthed nine children but found babies unpleasant from birth through that age when they still had a "big body and little limbs and that terrible frog-like action"—that is, until about four months old.

"I'm youth, I'm joy, I'm a little bird that has broken out of the egg!"

A David Copperfield

B Peter Pan

C Shirley Temple

D Tweety Bird

DID YOU KNOW?

For most birds, youth is quite brief. After hatching, a songbird typically leaves the nest in a matter of weeks.

ANSWER: B. The much-adored children's character has a number of magical abilities, but his most important feature is eternal youth. As J. M. Barrie writes in the first line of Peter Pan: "All children, except one, grow up."

"Who run the world? Girls."

 Lena Dunham

Ⓑ Beyoncé

Ⓒ Ian Fleming

Ⓓ Archie Andrews

 The number of women holding positions in national governments has doubled from the 1990s until today, but it still remains low. Female representatives make up only about a quarter of total elected leaders worldwide.

ANSWER: B. This is the chorus of Beyoncé's 2011 pop hit, "Run the World (Girls)." About nine months later, she had her own girl, Blue Ivy Carter.

"I only know two sorts of boys. Mealy boys, and beef-faced boys."

 A Jean-Jacques Rousseau

 B Florence Nightingale

C Charles Dickens

 D Theodore Roosevelt

COUNTER POINT

"There are two kinds of people in the world: the prickly and the gooey."

—ALAN WATTS

ANSWER: C. This line is spoken in Dickens's classic *Oliver Twist*, in which it is decided that our plucky protagonist Oliver is of the mealy variety.

"Please help me grow God. You know where. I want to be like everyone else."

A Louisa May Alcott

B Moll Flanders

C Anna Nicole Smith

D Margaret Simon
(*Are You There God? It's Me, Margaret*)

DID YOU KNOW?

Puberty is setting in earlier and earlier around the world. Though there is no clear explanation, scientists believe that environmental factors—including hormone-disrupting household chemicals—might be the culprits.

ANSWER: D. This plaintive prayer comes from Judy Blume's 1970 classic young adult novel about the anxiety of adolescence. Here, the protagonist relates that she has just told her mother she wants a bra.

"Of all animals the boy is the most unmanageable."

A Baloo (*The Jungle Book*)

B Plato

C Mary Poppins

D Charles Darwin

DID YOU KNOW?

The earliest known schools were established roughly 4,000 years ago in Mesopotamia for the instruction of writing and mathematics. Discipline was evidently harsh; anything from a word spoken out of turn to a writing mistake could warrant a flogging.

ANSWER: B. So Plato concludes in his late work *Laws*, which deals at one point with the education of children. The human boy is so troublesome, Plato writes, because "he has the fountain of reason in him not yet regulated."

"The Child is father of the Man."

A William Wordsworth

B Brian Wilson

C John the Baptist

D Jean Piaget

SEE ALSO:

"It takes a very long time to become young."

—PABLO PICASSO

ANSWER: A. This memorable axiom comes from Wordsworth's 1802 poem, "My Heart Leaps Up," it begins: "My heart leaps up when I behold/ A rainbow in the sky/ So was it when my life began/ So is it now I am a man."

"Who doesn't desire his father's death?"

A Oedipus Rex

B Fyodor Dostoyevsky

C Sigmund Freud

D Woody Allen

DID YOU KNOW?

The female version of the so-called Oedipus Complex—the supposed desire to kill one's father and marry one's mother—is called the Electra Complex, named for a Greek mythological character who plots with her brother to kill their mother, Clytemnestra.

ANSWER: B. Though this line seems like it was taken straight out of Freud, it actually occurs in Dostoyevsky's novel *The Brothers Karamazov*, spoken by a son whose father has been murdered.

"We don't need no education."

A Tom Sawyer

B Roger Waters

C Bobby Seale

D Sid Vicious

DID YOU KNOW?

Some early school leaders did hold a rather dim view of education. Said one prominent early-1900s educator: "Our schools are, in a sense, factories in which the raw products (children) are to be shaped and fashioned into products to meet the various demands of life."

ANSWER: B. This cry of youthful rebellion occurs in Pink Floyd's massive 1979 hit "Another Brick in the Wall (Part Two)" from their rock opera *The Wall*.

"Always obey your parents, when they are present."

A George Carlin

B Mark Twain

C Bart Simpson

D Ogden Nash

SEE ALSO:

"The thing that impresses me most about America is the way parents obey their children."

—KING EDWARD VIII

ANSWER: B. Twain included this nugget of wisdom in his sardonic 1882 "Address to Youth." He went on: "Most parents think they know better than you do, and you can generally make more by humoring that superstition than you can by acting on your own better judgment."

"There is no such thing as other people's children."

 A Angelina Jolie

B Hillary Clinton

C Hans Christian Andersen

D Jane Addams

FACT-CHECK There are roughly 2.2 billion children in the world—of whom most (if not all) are indeed other people's.

ANSWER: B. Clinton's interest in children's wellbeing was fully articulated in her book *It Takes a Village.* She attributed the book's title to an African proverb: "It takes a village to raise a child."

"Children have never been very good at listening to their elders, but they have never failed to imitate them."

 A James Baldwin

B F. Scott Fitzgerald

C Joseph P. Kennedy Sr.

D David Sedaris

COUNTER POINT

"The best way to give advice to your children is to find out what they want and then advise them to do it."

—HARRY S. TRUMAN

ANSWER: A. Baldwin was best known for his fierce social criticism and civil rights advocacy. But he also offered up incisive commentary on life and family, as in this line from the essay "Fifth Avenue, Uptown."

"I never had any friends later on like the ones I had when I was twelve. Jesus, does anyone?"

A Kevin Arnold
(*The Wonder Years*)

B Frank McCourt

C The Writer
(*Stand by Me*)

D Albert Camus

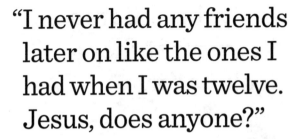

DID YOU KNOW?

Childhood friends are a gift indeed. Researchers have found that people who make close, long-lasting friendships in their youth are statistically less likely to have issues with anxiety or depression in adulthood.

ANSWER: C. These are the final lines spoken by the adult narrator in the cherished coming-of-age film *Stand by Me*, which was based on a novella by Stephen King about a group of boys searching for a missing body.

"Only the children know what they are looking for."

Ⓐ The Dalai Lama

Ⓑ Maria Montessori

Ⓒ Salvador Dalí

Ⓓ The Little Prince

SEE ALSO:

"There is frequently more to be learned from the unexpected questions of a child than the discourses of men."

—JOHN LOCKE

ANSWER: D. The eponymous subject of Antoine de Saint-Exupéry's 1943 story *The Little Prince* turns out to be a youthful interstellar traveler who encounters the narrator after the latter crash-lands in a desert.

"I cannot for the life of me understand why small children take so long to grow up. I think they do it deliberately, just to annoy me."

A Charlie Chaplin

B Jim Henson

C Agatha Trunchbull (*Matilda*)

D Joan Crawford

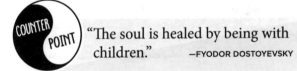

COUNTER POINT

"The soul is healed by being with children." —FYODOR DOSTOYEVSKY

ANSWER: C. The sadistic teacher from Roald Dahl's ageless childhood tale *Matilda*, Miss Trunchbull, even goes so far as to deny ever having been a child herself. This quotation derives from the film adaptation of the story.

"Adolescence is just one big walking pimple."

Ⓐ Kendall Jenner

Ⓑ J. D. Salinger

Ⓒ Carol Burnett

Ⓓ Gilda Radner

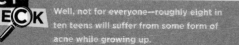

FACT-CHECK Well, not for everyone—roughly eight in ten teens will suffer from some form of acne while growing up.

ANSWER: C. The American television stalwart delivered this line in 1986 on *The Phil Donahue Show*, capturing one of the most salient—if least celebrated—facts of growing up.

"Who would ever think that so much can go on in the soul of a young girl?"

A Joan of Arc

B Hermione Granger
(Harry Potter series)

C Anne Frank

D Regan MacNeil
(*The Exorcist*)

DID YOU KNOW?

In 2006, two American scientists determined that children as young as four years old can indeed grasp the basic ontological significance of having a soul.

ANSWER: C. A Jewish girl who lived under Nazi occupation in Amsterdam in the 1940s, Frank wrote a personal diary that has come to be recognized as a unique testament to the human spirit.

"Adults are just obsolete children and the hell with them."

A Shelley Duvall

B Pee-wee Herman

C Raffi

D Dr. Seuss

DID YOU KNOW?

According to one notion of human evolution, called neoteny, there's some truth here. As the theory goes, humans evolved to carry youthful characteristics—such as curiosity and playfulness—into later stages of life. Perhaps we really are young at heart!

ANSWER: D. Dr. Seuss—real name Theodor Geisel—wrote some of the most beloved picture books in the English language, including *Oh, the Places You'll Go!* and *The Cat in the Hat.* He had no patience for writing for adults, however.

"I don't wish to cling to youth. I can't help that youth clings to me."

A Dorian Gray (*The Picture of Dorian Gray*)

B Fred Savage

C Pamela Anderson

D Mickey Rooney

> **SEE ALSO:**
>
> "We are all born mad.
> Some remain so."
>
> —SAMUEL BECKETT

ANSWER: C. In 2018, this apparently original line appeared, without explanation, on the actress and former *Playboy* model's website, pamelaandersonfoundation.org.

"Life moves pretty fast. If you don't stop and look around once in a while, you could miss it."

 A Bill Murray

B Ferris Bueller

C James Dean

D John Updike

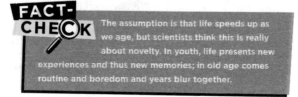

FACT-CHECK The assumption is that life speeds up as we age, but scientists think this is really about novelty. In youth, life presents new experiences and thus new memories; in old age comes routine and boredom and years blur together.

ANSWER: B. John Hughes's 1986 comedy *Ferris Bueller's Day Off* quickly became a cultural touchstone. In 1990, First Lady Barbara Bush even quoted this line in a commencement address—to roaring applause.

"He not busy being born is busy dying."

A Michelangelo

B Amelia Earhart

C Confucius

D Bob Dylan

COUNTER POINT

"Not to be born at all is best."

—SOPHOCLES

ANSWER: D. Born Robert Zimmerman, Dylan changed rock and roll indelibly with his aphoristic lyrics and signature vocal delivery. This proverb comes from his 1965 track "It's Alright, Ma (I'm Only Bleeding)."

"My mama always said, 'life was like a box of chocolates. You never know what you're gonna get.'"

A Milton S. Hershey

B Raymond Babbitt (*Rain Man*)

C Shel Silverstein

D Forrest Gump

DID YOU KNOW?

The largest box of chocolates ever made was a Thorntons Moments box, produced by Thorntons and Russell Beck Studios, weighing 3,725 pounds, or nearly two tons.

ANSWER: D. This is the signature line in the movie adaptation of Winston Groom's 1986 novel. The original line, which opens the book, is somewhat less saccharine: "Let me say this: bein a idiot is no box of chocolates."

"Teenage angst has paid off well. Now I'm bored and old."

A Kurt Cobain

....

B Neil Young

....

C Miley Cyrus

D Holden Caulfield

....

WORD UP

The word "angst" didn't become common in the English language until translations of Freud popularized its usage in the 1920s. It has since become a common descriptor of moody adolescents.

ANSWER: A. Perhaps the most accomplished communicator of modern teenage angst, the late Nirvana frontman forged a new type of "cool" for young people in the 1990s.

"My advice to myself and to everyone else, particularly young people, is to turn on, tune in, and drop out."

Ⓐ Jerry Garcia

Ⓑ Jack Nicholson

Ⓒ Joan Didion

Ⓓ Timothy Leary

SEE ALSO:

"Blessed youth, launch your boat and fly from every form of education."

—EPICURUS

ANSWER: D. An advocate of recreational LSD use, Leary became a leading figure of the 1960s American counterculture movement. Richard Nixon once described him as "the most dangerous man in America."

GROWING UP

28

"Go West, young man."

A Horace Greeley

B James K. Polk

C Laura Ingalls Wilder

D Daniel Boone

DID YOU KNOW?

Given the scant female population on the frontier, "Go West, young woman" might have been better advice. The 1850 census in California, for instance, found the population to be more than 90 percent male.

ANSWER: A. The nineteenth-century writer and newspaper editor is widely credited with dispensing this famous piece of advice, which encapsulated the pioneering spirit of American westward expansion.

"One is not born, but rather becomes, a woman."

A Sophia Loren

B Georgia O'Keeffe

C Simone de Beauvoir

D Germaine Greer

SEE ALSO:

"Who in the world am I? Ah, that's the great puzzle."

—ALICE (*Alice in Wonderland*)

ANSWER: C. This oft-quoted line, from de Beauvoir's 1949 masterwork *The Second Sex*, relates to her signature theory of woman as an "other," in a male-dominated society.

"Whatever else is unsure in this stinking dunghill of a world a mother's love is not."

A John Lennon

B James Joyce

C Jackie Gleason

D "Ma" Jarrett (*White Heat*)

DID YOU KNOW?

Humans aren't the only species with impressive moms. A giant Pacific octopus mother, for instance, guards her eggs so devotedly that, if starving, she will resort to eating her own arms in lieu of leaving the eggs to find food.

ANSWER: B. This line appears in the Irish literary great's first novel, *A Portrait of the Artist as a Young Man*, a semi-autobiographical coming-of-age story that draws from Joyce's conflicted relationship with his mother.

FINISH
THE
QUOTE

Kanye West,
to Taylor Swift:
"Imma let you—"

DIFFICULTY LEVEL

President Franklin Delano Roosevelt said the following. Can you finish the quote?

"The only thing we have to fear is—"

 A . . . utter failure.

B . . . fear itself.

C . . . a surprise attack on one of our Pacific military bases.

D . . . Communism.

ANSWER: B. Roosevelt spoke these immortal words at his first inauguration in 1933, the height of the Great Depression. Said the new president: "This great Nation will endure as it has endured, will revive and will prosper."

Jeff "The Dude" Lebowski, the protagonist of the Coen brothers' cult film *The Big Lebowski*, said the following. Can you finish the quote?

"The Dude—"

 **...** persists.

B . . . is dead.

C . . . abides.

D . . . is done.

ANSWER: C. This is the final line spoken by Jeff Bridges as the Dude. The charmingly spaced-out character has inspired several pop-philosophy books, including *The Tao of the Dude* and *The Abide Guide: Living Like Lebowski*.

British author **Jane Austen**, wrote the following.
Can you finish the quote?

"It is a truth universally acknowledged, that a single man in possession of a good fortune, must—"

A ... be in want of a wife.

B ... have committed a great crime.

C ... ever peer over his shoulder.

D ... don only the finest breeches.

ANSWER: A. Austen begins her 1813 novel *Pride and Prejudice* with this sentence, which sets the stage for a subtle comedy of manners revolving around questions of marriage, love, and—crucially—money.

American poet **T. S. Eliot** wrote the following.
Can you finish the quote?

"Immature poets imitate. Mature poets—."

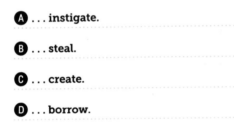

A . . . instigate.

B . . . steal.

C . . . create.

D . . . borrow.

ANSWER: B. Eliot's dictum was later echoed in a favorite saying of Steve Jobs's—"Good artists copy; great artists steal." Ironically, Jobs misattributed the saying to Pablo Picasso.

Ronaldo Luís Nazário de Lima, the Brazilian soccer legend—known simply as **Ronaldo**—said the following. Can you finish the quote?

"We lost because we didn't—"

A . . . win.

B . . . pray.

C . . . score.

D . . . feel like winning.

ANSWER: A. As the three-time FIFA World Player of the Year made clear, sometimes winning is just a matter of not losing—and vice versa.

MINI-GAME: FINISH THE QUOTE

38

Laurel Thatcher Ulrich, a Harvard University historian and author, said the following. Can you finish the quote?

"Well-behaved women seldom—"

A . . . behave well.

B . . . disappoint their fathers.

C . . . make history.

D . . . find suitable mates.

ANSWER: C. This adage—now the stuff of bumper stickers and T-shirts— originated in an obscure scholarly article Ulrich penned in 1976 on the traditional portrayals of women in Christian funeral rites.

DIFFICULTY LEVEL

World-renowned physicist **Albert Einstein** said the following. Can you finish the quote?

"God does not—"

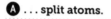

Ⓐ . . . split atoms.

Ⓑ . . . know E=mc².

Ⓒ . . . create or destroy energy.

Ⓓ . . . play dice with the universe.

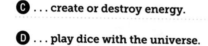

ANSWER: D. This famous quote relates Einstein's skepticism about quantum physics, a theory that presumes a fundamental randomness at the heart of the physical world. "The theory yields much," Einstein wrote, "but it hardly brings us closer to the Old One's secrets."

Secretary of State **Hillary Clinton** said the following. Can you finish the quote?

"If I didn't _____ every day, he wouldn't be worth anything."

A . . . tell Bill I loved him . . .

B . . . kick Bill Clinton's ass . . .

C . . . give my husband a pep talk . . .

D . . . get Bill a Big Mac . . .

ANSWER: B. This is what Clinton once told an aide about her unique relationship with husband Bill, to whom she has been married since 1975.

President George H. W. Bush said the following.
Can you finish the quote?

"I'm President of the United States and I'm not going to—"

A . . . France.

B . . . take Pepto-Bismol.

C . . . eat any more broccoli.

D . . . answer any more dumb questions.

ANSWER: C. When it was reported that the cruciferous vegetable was banned from Air Force One, Bush gave an explanation that picky toddlers the world over would appreciate.

Media theorist **Marshall McLuhan** said the following. Can you finish the quote?

"The medium is the—"

A ... message.

B ... master.

C ... mother.

D ... man.

ANSWER: A. First appearing in the 1964 book *Understanding Media: The Extensions of Man*, McLuhan's phrase suggests that a medium (the written word, television, radio, etc.) embeds itself into the message being conveyed.

MINI-GAME: FINISH THE QUOTE

43

American poet and musician **Gil Scott-Heron** said the following. Can you finish the quote?

"The revolution will not be—"

A . . . a trail of roses.

B . . . a tea party.

C . . . bought.

D . . . televised.

ANSWER: D. This line appeared on the spoken-word artist's subversive 1970 debut, *Small Talk at 125th and Lenox*. Scott-Heron's work was instrumental to the genesis of rap, although the artist himself denied it.

Blanche DuBois, the protagonist of *A Streetcar Named Desire*, said the following. Can you finish the quote?

"I have always depended on—"

A . . . the folly of men.

B . . . the kindness of strangers.

C . . . the vagaries of fortune.

D . . . the grace of God.

ANSWER: B. DuBois delivers her discordant final line in the play—and subsequent film version—as she is hauled off to a New Orleans mental institution, having lost touch with reality in a fog of grief and drink.

President Abraham Lincoln said the following.
Can you finish the quote?

"The mystic chords of memory, stretching from every battlefield and patriot grave to every living heart and hearthstone all over this broad land, will yet swell the chorus of the Union, when again touched, as surely they will be, by—"

Ⓐ . . . the audacity of hope.

Ⓑ . . . the slings and arrows of outrageous fortune.

Ⓒ . . . the better angels of our nature.

Ⓓ . . . the arc of the moral universe.

ANSWER: C. Lincoln's 1861 inaugural address, which was preceded by the secession of seven southern states from the Union, contained a message of hope for reunification.

French existentialist **Jean-Paul Sartre** wrote the
following. Can you finish the quote?

"Hell is—"

A ... ourselves.

B ... empty and all the devils are here.

C ... paved with good intentions.

D ... other people.

ANSWER: D. So concludes one of the three characters in Sartre's existentialist play *No Exit*, in which strangers are trapped in a small room together for eternity. As one of them surmises, "There's no need for red-hot pokers."

Irina Dunn, an Australian writer and politician, wrote the following. Can you finish the quote?

"A woman needs a man like—"

A . . . a man needs a woman.

B . . . the desert needs the rain.

C . . . a fish needs a bicycle.

D . . . a brain needs a bullet.

ANSWER: C. Though it has been misattributed to women like Gloria Steinem and Erica Jong, the quip has its roots in a piece of graffiti Dunn penned on Sydney toilet stalls in the early 1970s.

Ralph Waldo Emerson, the American transcendentalist writer and philosopher, wrote the following. Can you finish the quote?

"Hitch your wagon to a—"

A ... dream.

B ... bigger wagon.

C ... stallion.

D ... star.

ANSWER: D. Now the stuff of motivational posters, this line occurs in Emerson's 1862 essay "Civilization," a work concerned less with individual striving than the way entire nations rise and progress.

LOVE & MARRIAGE

"All You Need
Is Love."

—THE BEATLES

"You had me at hello."

A Tammy Wynette

B Dorothy Boyd (*Jerry Maguire*)

C Mrs. Robinson (*The Graduate*)

D Jane Eyre

DID YOU KNOW?

A person's voice is more important to human mating than you might think. One study that measured the perceived attractiveness of different voices found that hotter-sounding voices tended to come from conventionally well-proportioned people.

ANSWER: B. It's a classic line, but one rarely quoted in full. Just after Tom Cruise says, "You complete me," Renee Zellweger cuts him off, "Just shut up—you had me at hello."

"Love is three minutes of squelching noises."

A James Joyce

B Ambrose Bierce

C Johnny Rotten (John Lydon)

D Valerie Solanas

SEE ALSO:

"How alike are the groans of love, to those of the dying."

—MALCOLM LOWRY

ANSWER: C. This is also an accurate description of most songs from Rotten's punk band, the Sex Pistols, whose 1977 single "God Save the Queen" was among the most controversial—and banned—songs in British history.

"Thank God I'm in love again. Now I can do it for love and not for my complexion."

A Joan Crawford

B Freddie Mercury

C Barbara Stanwyck

D Carrie Bradshaw
(*Sex and the City*)

DID YOU KNOW?

Regular sexual activity has been associated with a wide range of positive health benefits, including reduced stress, better immune system function, and even pain relief.

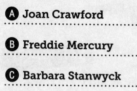

ANSWER: A. The Hollywood icon was known for her passionate performances in films like *Grand Hotel* and *Mildred Pierce*. Crawford reportedly delivered this droll line during her marriage to actor and frequent costar Franchot Tone.

"In my sex fantasy, nobody ever loves me for my mind."

 A Joan Rivers

 B Richard Feynman

 C Nora Ephron

D Bea Arthur

FACT-CHECK In recent years, a niche community has emerged calling themselves "sapiosexuals"—that is, people attracted to intelligence. Though the concept is controversial, it has already achieved one important measure of validation: a dating app for sapiosexuals.

ANSWER: C. Ephron, who began her career as a journalist, wrote several iconic romantic comedies, including *Sleepless in Seattle* and *When Harry Met Sally.*

"Lord, give me chastity and self-control—but not just yet."

A William S. Burroughs

B Odysseus

C Saint Augustine

D Marquis de Sade

DID YOU KNOW?

Though we have a modern image of women being forced to wear clunky, locking chastity belts in the Middle Ages, it's likely a myth. What did really exist, however, in the nineteenth century, were intricate devices designed to discourage self-pleasure.

ANSWER: C. This prayer (of sorts) comes from the fourth-century Christian theologian's thirteen-volume autobiography, titled *Confessions*, which described his lustful youth and eventual religious conversion.

"I want you to draw me like one of your French girls."

Ⓐ Edie Sedgwick

Ⓑ Rose (*Titanic*)

Ⓒ Françoise Gilot

Ⓓ Georgia O'Keeffe

DID YOU KNOW?

Due to concerns over impropriety, female models were rarely used for Renaissance nudes. When a female subject was required, as in Raphael's *Alba Madonna*, artists often painted from a male model and then made necessary anatomical adjustments.

ANSWER: B. Perhaps the most memorable piece of dialog from the 1997 smash hit *Titanic*, this seductive line is delivered by Kate Winslet to Leonardo DiCaprio, just before he paints her in the "French" style—that's to say, nude.

"If I had to count my sexual encounters, I would be closing in on twenty thousand women. Yes, that's correct—twenty thousand different ladies."

A Wilt Chamberlain

B Warren Beatty

C Gene Simmons

D Fidel Castro

This is equivalent to having a different partner every night for about fifty-five years. Sounds complicated.

ANSWER: A. Seven-foot-one Wilt Chamberlain was known for scoring in more ways than one. He still holds the record for most points scored in a single game—100.

"When women go wrong, men go right after them."

A Mae West

B Billy Graham

C Phyllis Diller

D Emily Post

COUNTER POINT

"You treat a dame like a lady, and you treat a lady like a dame."

—FRANK SINATRA, in *Pal Joey*

ANSWER: A. Though the classic Hollywood star often attracted controversy, her real legacy was her phenomenal wit. "When I'm good, I'm very, very good," West once said, "But when I'm bad, I'm better."

"What's in a name? That which we call a rose by any other name would smell as sweet."

 A Samuel Pepys

B William Shakespeare

C Michelangelo

 D Percy Bysshe Shelley

SEE ALSO:

"A rose is a rose is a rose."

—GERTRUDE STEIN

ANSWER: B. This indelible line, spoken by Juliet in the tragedy *Romeo and Juliet*, refers to the fact that Romeo is of the Montague family, and thus a sworn enemy of Juliet's Capulet clan. No word on how Romeo smelled.

"I'd do anything for love but I won't do that."

A Hall and Oates

B Dave Chappelle

C Meat Loaf

D Humphrey Bogart

DID YOU KNOW?

There is one thing that at least a third of millennials won't do for love: give up on a $37,000 raise. That was one conclusion of a recent survey, which also found that about 40 percent of millennials would end a relationship for a big promotion.

ANSWER: C. Meat Loaf's 1993 mega-hit has long vexed listeners. But don't let your imagination run wild. As Meat Loaf explained, each "that" referred to a previous lyric.

"You need kissing badly. That's what's wrong with you. You should be kissed and often, and by someone who knows how."

A Rick Blaine (*Casablanca*)

B Ernest Hemingway

C Ella Fitzgerald

D Rhett Butler (*Gone with the Wind*)

DID YOU KNOW?

Locking lips actually entails real health benefits. For example, couples engaged in longer smooches (over ten seconds) will transfer some 80 million bacteria between them. While that may sound risky, a diverse oral microbiome is actually pretty good for you.

ANSWER: D. Played by Clark Gable, Butler delivers this tantalizing line to love interest Scarlett O'Hara (Vivien Leigh). But Gable's most famous line from the movie was the then-controversial "Frankly, my dear, I don't give a damn."

"Love conquers all things."

 A Homer

 B Anne Boleyn

 C George Eliot

 D Virgil

COUNTER POINT

"Love conquers all things except poverty and toothache."

—MAE WEST (popularized by)

ANSWER: D. This enduring maxim is just one of many that trace back to the Roman poet. Other Virgilian all-time hits include "Fortune favors the bold" and *E pluribus unum.*

"If it weren't for lies, there'd be no sex."

A Andrea Dworkin

B Giacomo Casanova

C Jerry Seinfeld

D Morrissey

DID YOU KNOW?

It was ever thus. Greek mythology is full of gods deceiving their way into bed. In one example, Zeus disguised himself as a friendly white bull in order to seduce the mortal Europa, only revealing his true form after they were secluded on an island.

ANSWER: C. According to the stand-up comedy great, duplicity is part and parcel of human sexuality. "Everyone lies about sex," Seinfeld said. "People lie *during* sex."

"It was love at first sight, at last sight, at ever and ever sight."

Ⓐ Nora Roberts

Ⓑ Emily Brontë

Ⓒ Edith Wharton

Ⓓ Vladimir Nabokov

COUNTER POINT

"I believe in love at first sight for houses—but not for people."

—DANIELLE STEEL

ANSWER: D. A tender sentiment, sure, but less so in the context of Nabokov's novel *Lolita*, the story of a man who becomes sexually involved—read: commits statutory rape—with a twelve-year-old girl.

"There is always some madness in love. But there is always, also, some reason in madness."

A Jacqueline Kennedy Onassis

B Marlon Brando

C Anne Sexton

D Friedrich Nietzsche

SEE ALSO:

"Love: A temporary insanity curable by marriage."

—AMBROSE BIERCE

ANSWER: D. This line is among the many aphorisms in Nietzsche's confounding masterpiece *Thus Spake Zarathustra*. Another: "It is true we love life; not because we are wont to live, but because we are wont to love."

"A man in love is incomplete until he has married—then he's finished."

A Zsa Zsa Gabor

B Lucille Ball

C Orson Welles

D H. L. Mencken

DID YOU KNOW?

Married men are, on average, three pounds heavier than their bachelor counterparts. That's just more to love!

ANSWER: A. Married nine times, the Hungarian-born actress and socialite was a star of both the silver screen and the gossip pages. Among her many notable dalliances was a purported blind date with Henry Kissinger.

"I married beneath me—all women do."

A Roseanne Barr

B Ava Gardner

C Nancy Astor

D Cleopatra

FACT-CHECK

There may be some truth to this. American women are more likely on average than men to initiate divorces.

ANSWER: C. Born in Virginia, the future Mrs. Astor had wedded an alcoholic at age 18 before divorcing, expatriating to England, and marrying into the famously wealthy Astor family. Later she became the first female member of Parliament to take her seat.

LOVE & MARRIAGE

68

"I think that gay marriage is something that should be between a man and a woman."

A Arnold Schwarzenegger

B Fred Phelps, founder of the Westboro Baptist Church

C George W. Bush

D Pope John Paul II

COUNTER POINT

"I support gay marriage because I believe they have every right to be just as miserable as the rest of us."

—KINKY FRIEDMAN

ANSWER: A. The actor and former bodybuilder made a bit of a gaffe while describing his position on same-sex marriage in his campaign for governor of California. In office, however, he officiated at two gay weddings.

"How do I love thee? Let me count the ways."

A Geoffrey Chaucer

B Elizabeth Barrett Browning

C Giovanni Boccaccio

D Napoleon Bonaparte

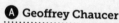

DID YOU KNOW?

According to dating site OkCupid, most successful new couples agree on three questions: 1) "Do you like horror movies?" 2) "Have you ever traveled around another country alone?" and 3) "Wouldn't it be fun to chuck it all and go live on a sailboat?"

ANSWER: B. This occurs in one of Browning's "Sonnets from the Portuguese," published in 1850. The poem doesn't waste any time with subtlety: "I love thee to the depth and breadth and height / My soul can reach."

"I would rather be a beggar and single than a queen and married."

 Betty Friedan

 Jane Austen

 Queen Elizabeth I

 Diane Keaton

COUNTER POINT

"Reader, I married him."

—JANE EYRE

ANSWER: C. The Virgin Queen reportedly was referring to a suitor's attempts at courtship. "When I think of marriage," she was quoted elsewhere, "it is as though my heart were being dragged out of my vitals."

"All happy families resemble one another; each unhappy family is unhappy in its own way."

A Ann Landers

B Christina Crawford

C John Steinbeck

D Leo Tolstoy

DID YOU KNOW?

America is unique among developed countries in how much happier non-parents are compared to parents. In other English-speaking countries and Europe, the so-called happiness gap is smaller, non-existent, or even reversed.

ANSWER: D. The Russian novelist made the sorrows and joys of family life one of his central preoccupations. This line begins his magnum opus *Anna Karenina*.

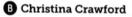

"There were three of us in this marriage, so it was a bit crowded."

A Diana, Princess of Wales

B Mia Farrow

C Sandra Bullock

D Maria Shriver

SEE ALSO:

"I could sooner reconcile all Europe than two women."

—KING LOUIS XIV

ANSWER: A. This was Princess Di's bombshell reaction when asked in a **1995 television interview** about her husband Prince Charles's infidelity. The remarks scandalized England, and within a year they were divorced.

"Hearts will never be practical until they can be made unbreakable."

A Ingmar Bergman

B Carl Sagan

C Oprah Winfrey

D The Wizard of Oz

SEE ALSO:

"Having a pulmonary embolism is definitely a lot easier than heartbreak."

—SERENA WILLIAMS

ANSWER: D. This is the Wizard's warning to the Tin Man, who yearns for a heart. Instead, he gets a pocket watch and some advice: "A heart is not judged by how much you love, but by how much you are loved by others."

"I'd marry again if I found a man who had fifteen million dollars, would sign over half to me, and guarantee that he'd be dead within a year."

A Cher

B Anna Nicole Smith

C Bette Davis

D Kathy Griffin

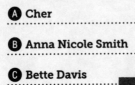

DID YOU KNOW?

Money plays a larger role in marital success than we may like to believe. According to a study conducted in 2018, the more unequal two spouses's incomes are, the more likely they are to separate.

ANSWER: C. The Golden-Age Hollywood actress commanded a larger-than-life presence, both on screen and off. She was married four times in all.

DIFFICULTY LEVEL

"'Tis better to have loved and lost than never to have loved at all."

 Alfred, Lord Tennyson

B John Milton

C Christina Rossetti

D Dante Alighieri

"Love is so short, forgetting is so long."

—PABLO NERUDA

ANSWER: A. Tennyson penned this memorable verse in his plaintive *In Memoriam A.H.H.*, which, far from being a romantic lyric, mourns the early death of a platonic friend.

"Some of us are becoming the men we wanted to marry."

A Camille Paglia

B Victoria Woodhull, free love advocate and first woman to run for US president

C Gloria Steinem

D Cyndi Lauper

SEE ALSO:

"I do not wish [women] to have power over men; but over themselves."

—MARY WOLLSTONECRAFT

ANSWER: C. Steinem's pugnacious journalism played a key role in feminism's second wave during the 1960s. The story that made her famous involved going undercover as a Playboy Bunny.

"It's a nice day for a white wedding."

A Blondie

B Billy Idol

C Miss Havisham
(*Great Expectations*)

D Boy George

DID YOU KNOW?

It was only relatively recently that a white dress became basically de rigueur for Anglo American brides. The turning point came with the ornate white satin gown Queen Victoria wore in her wedding in 1840, which caused an international sensation.

ANSWER: B. Idol's 1982 hit got inspiration from his sister, who had recently been wed while pregnant. In reality, Idol was happy for her, but in the song he was enraged at the taboo of a shotgun wedding.

"Love consists in this, that two solitudes protect and touch and greet each other."

A Anaïs Nin

B Rainer Maria Rilke

C Elena Ferrante

D Erich Fromm

"Love is a snowmobile racing across the tundra and then suddenly it flips over, pinning you underneath. At night, the ice weasels come."

—MATT GROENING,
creator of *The Simpsons*

ANSWER: B. Though Rilke was a major German poet of the early twentieth century, he may be best known today for his *Letters to a Young Poet*, a series of correspondences with a young bard on the intricacies of love and art.

"I wish I knew how to quit you."

A Chris Kraus

B George Strait

C Cathy Earnshaw (*Wuthering Heights*)

D Jack Twist (*Brokeback Mountain*)

SEE ALSO:

"Love will tear us apart."

—IAN CURTIS,
Joy Division

ANSWER: D. The 2005 hit *Brokeback Mountain* told the saga of secret love between two Wyoming cowboys. The film ignited a cultural firestorm, with warnings that the movie attempted to "mainstream homosexual conduct."

"Nobody dies from lack of sex. It's lack of love we die from."

A E. L. James

B Ruth Westheimer

C Margaret Atwood

D Mother Teresa

> **DID YOU KNOW?**
>
> People tend to associate sex with happiness: the more the merrier. But when scientists in 2015 instructed couples to make twice as much love as usual for one month, the test subjects actually reported being less happy. Apparently, less is more.

ANSWER: C. Atwood's novel *The Handmaid's Tale*, from which this quotation derives, describes a dystopian future in which a totalitarian theocracy rules over America, subjecting fertile women to a form of sexual slavery.

OUT OF CONTEXT

"It depends on what the meaning of the word 'is' is."

—BILL CLINTON

WHAT WERE THEY
YAPPIN' ABOUT?

"If you still have to ask, shame on you."

—LOUIS ARMSTRONG

A On whether it really is a wonderful world

B On what "jazz" is

C On what a "jazz cigarette" is

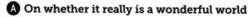

ANSWER: B. Sometimes misquoted as "Man, if you gotta ask, you'll never know," this line was just one of the legendary trumpeter's many quips. "All music is folk music," he once said. "I ain't never heard no horse sing a song."

**WHAT WERE THEY
YAPPIN' ABOUT?**

"... merely the scratching of pimples on the body of the bootboy at Claridges."

—VIRGINIA WOOLF

Ⓐ On Igor Stravinsky's *The Rite of Spring*

Ⓑ On T. S. Eliot's *The Waste Land*

Ⓒ On James Joyce's *Ulysses*

ANSWER: C. Joyce's 1922 magnum opus set the literary world ablaze, but reaction was sharply divided. Woolf was a fellow modernist and an exact contemporary of Joyce's (both lived 1882–1941), yet she was no fan.

WHAT WERE THEY
YAPPIN' ABOUT?

"Red meat and gin."

—JULIA CHILD

A On what a young woman should serve a man on a dinner date

B On the worst pairing she'd ever been served

C On what accounted for her longevity

ANSWER: C. The French chef championed rich, buttery cooking in a time of increasing nutrition awareness and fat-phobia. "The only time to eat diet food is while you're waiting for the steak to cook," she once declared.

WHAT WERE THEY YAPPIN' ABOUT?

"We're heading into nut country today."

—JOHN F. KENNEDY

A On making a 1960 campaign stop in Dougherty County, Georgia, the largest pecan producer in the US

B On sending the first armed troops into Vietnam

C On arriving in Dallas on November 22, 1963

ANSWER: C. Kennedy uttered this on the day of his assassination. The last words reportedly spoken to Kennedy before shots rang out came from a member of his motorcade: "You can't say Dallas doesn't love you, Mr. President."

WHAT WERE THEY
YAPPIN' ABOUT?

"I have sinned against my brother, the ass."

—SAINT FRANCIS OF ASSISI

Ⓐ On accidentally leaving his donkey out during a light rain

Ⓑ On his failing body, while on his deathbed

Ⓒ On being accused of drinking a fellow friar's wine

ANSWER: B. These dying words are attributed to the twelfth-century Catholic saint. Francis's tireless work came at the expense of his health, however, and he reportedly regretted neglecting his body—or as he called it, "the ass."

WHAT WERE THEY
YAPPIN' ABOUT?

"I can't really remember the names of the clubs that we went to."

—SHAQUILLE O'NEAL

A On the teams he played against in the 2000 NBA playoffs

B On the itinerary for a charity tour of Boys & Girls Clubs of America

C On whether he had visited the Parthenon while in Greece

ANSWER: C. Shaq's nickname—The Big Aristotle—is meant somewhat ironically. The Parthenon, built roughly 2,500 years ago, is one of the best-known ruins in Athens.

**WHAT WERE THEY
YAPPIN' ABOUT?**

"It is a tale told by an idiot, full of sound and fury, signifying nothing."
—WILLIAM SHAKESPEARE

A On life (*Macbeth*)

B On *The Tragical History of the Life and Death of Doctor Faustus*, a tragedy written by Shakespeare's rival, Christopher Marlowe

C On Hamlet's "To be, or not to be" monologue, according to Ophelia (*Hamlet*)

ANSWER: A. So ends one of Shakespeare's best-known soliloquies "Life's but a walking shadow," the unhinged Scottish king laments, "a poor player that struts and frets his hour upon the stage and then is heard no more."

WHAT WERE THEY YAPPIN' ABOUT?

"There is no there there."

—GERTRUDE STEIN

A On Oakland, California

....

B On heterosexuality

....

C On Ezra Pound's poetry

....

ANSWER: A. The modernist writer coined this idiom in *Everybody's Autobiography*, a follow-up to her surprisingly successful (and misleadingly titled memoir) *The Autobiography of Alice B. Toklas*.

MINI-GAME: OUT OF CONTEXT

91

"It's like kissing Hitler."

—TONY CURTIS

 On being punched in the face while training for the boxing movie *Flesh and Fury*

 On his addiction to cocaine

 On kissing Marilyn Monroe

ANSWER: C. Curtis once said the jab was a mere joke; other times it was reported to be the result of friction on the set of *Some Like It Hot* between him and Monroe, whom he had briefly dated before they were famous (or so he claimed).

WHAT WERE THEY
YAPPIN' ABOUT?

"Clearly, mistakes were made."

—GEORGE H. W. BUSH

A On vomiting on the prime minister of Japan

B On the Reagan administration selling weapons to Iran to finance an illegal war in Nicaragua

C On raising taxes two years after making the famous pledge: "Read my lips: no new taxes"

ANSWER: B. This was how the then–vice president characterized the Iran-Contra scandal engulfing the Reagan administration. Bush's son would later echo these words following revelations of abuses by US forces in Iraq.

WHAT WERE THEY
YAPPIN' ABOUT?

"Feet—why do I need them if I have wings to fly?"

—FRIDA KAHLO

 A On taking her first voyage by airplane, to New York City

B On the amputation of her right leg

C After being told her feet were too large for her to be a model

ANSWER: B. The Mexican artist had numerous health issues throughout her life, including the removal of part of her right leg due to gangrene. These words appeared in her diary beneath a drawing of her disembodied legs sprouting vines.

"The die is cast."

—JULIUS CAESAR

A On the day of his assassination by Marcus Junius Brutus and others

B On crossing the Rubicon river, precipitating the Roman civil war

C On completing the conquest of Gaul

ANSWER: B. Caesar uttered these fateful words upon leading his forces into Rome, where he had been ordered to return sans army. Despite Caesar having only one legion, the gambit eventually propelled him to dictatorship.

"They are useless. They can only give you answers."

—PABLO PICASSO

 A On computers

 B On dictionaries

 C On priests

ANSWER: A. Given that Picasso was known for breaking with convention and depicting the impossible, it makes sense that this quotation, recorded in 1964, shows him once again ahead of his time.

"Today I consider myself
the luckiest man on
the face of the earth."

—LOU GEHRIG

A On breaking the record for most consecutive
games played

B On retiring due to terminal illness

C On having a new style of ballpark frank named
after him

ANSWER: B. Two weeks after being forced into retirement by the onset of
amyotrophic lateral sclerosis—now known as Lou Gehrig's disease—the
slugger delivered this heartfelt goodbye to more than 60,000 Yankee fans.

"I had the radio on."

—MARILYN MONROE

 A On reports of strange sounds emanating
from her and Joe DiMaggio's hotel suite

B On how she heard about her reputed former
lover John F. Kennedy's assassination

C On being asked if she had posed with
nothing on during a 1949 photoshoot

ANSWER: C. In the early 1950s, controversy swirled around the rising starlet, who had recently posed for pin-ups in the nude—a scandal for Hollywood actresses of that time.

**WHAT WERE THEY
YAPPIN' ABOUT?**

"Anyone who isn't
confused doesn't
really understand the
situation." —EDWARD R. MURROW

A On the Vietnam War

B On the Nixon impeachment

C On the breakup of the Beatles

ANSWER: A. This was how the iconic newscaster reportedly described the escalating war in Vietnam in the 1960s. With ominous insights like that, it's no wonder his nightly catchphrase was "Good night and good luck."

WORK
&
MONEY

"It costs a lot
of money to look
this cheap."

—DOLLY PARTON

"All paid employments ...absorb and degrade the mind."

A Aristotle

B Emma Goldman

C Leo Tolstoy

D George Washington

When it comes to motivation, hard cash may not be all it's cracked up to be. For complex tasks, researchers have found that money incentives are not always great motivators. In fact, jumbo prizes may even be a drag on performance.

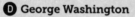

ANSWER: A. The ancient philosophers valued work far less than we moderns do. Aristotle said elsewhere that "citizens must not lead the life of mechanics or tradesmen, for such a life is ignoble and inimical to virtue."

"I'm not a businessman, I'm a business, man."

A Charles Foster Kane (*Citizen Kane*)

B Jay-Z

C Stewart Brand

D Russell Simmons

COUNTER POINT "Man's life is not a business."

—SAUL BELLOW

ANSWER: B. Shawn Carter (aka Jay-Z) launched Roc-A-Fella Records in 1995, and has since built a business empire spanning music, fashion, real estate, tech, and beyond. The original Rockefeller would be proud.

"We don't have a lot of time on this Earth! We weren't meant to spend it this way! Human beings were not meant to sit in little cubicles staring at computer screens all day filling out useless forms and listening to eight different bosses drone on about mission statements."

 A Michael Scott (*The Office*)

B Peter Gibbons (*Office Space*)

C Steve Wozniak

D Dilbert

SEE ALSO:

"I would prefer not to."
—BARTLEBY, THE SCRIVENER
(Herman Melville)

ANSWER: B. Mike Judge's 1999 film has assumed cult status for its pitiless deconstruction of American office drudgery. As the slacker protagonist muses at one point: "It's not that I'm lazy—it's that I just don't care."

"A large income is the best recipe for happiness I ever heard of."

A Martha Stewart

B Jane Austen

C J. Paul Getty

D Jay Gatsby
(*The Great Gatsby*)

SEE ALSO:

"Money is better than poverty, if only for financial reasons."

—WOODY ALLEN

ANSWER: B. In the Austen novel *Mansfield Park*, young men and women navigate the perilous terrains of class and romance in and around a posh country estate. This line is spoken by a fashionable young woman, Mary, to a male suitor known *not* to have much of an income.

"I've been in the twilight of my career longer than most people have had their career."

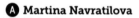

A Martina Navratilova

B Michael Jordan

C Barbra Streisand

D Jerry Stiller

DID YOU KNOW?

Certain careers do tilt toward the elderly. According to *Time* magazine, the top three oldest types of worker are a motley bunch: tax preparer, clergy member, and farmer.

ANSWER: A. After winning an astounding eighteen Grand Slam singles titles and an all-time record thirty-one major doubles titles, the Czechoslovakian-born tennis star became an outspoken activist for gay rights and animal welfare.

"There's nothing in the world so demoralizing as money."

A F. Scott Fitzgerald

B Sophocles

C Mahatma Gandhi

D Edie Sedgwick

SEE ALSO:

"Money doesn't talk, it swears."

—BOB DYLAN

ANSWER: B. The Greek playwright penned this line in *Antigone*. Here, a king laments that one of his guards has been bribed.

"It is not from the benevolence of the butcher, the brewer, or the baker that we expect our dinner, but from their regard to their own interest."

A David Hume

B Friedrich Engels

C Adam Smith

D Benjamin Franklin

WORD UP

There's a reason why *interest* can refer to a financial payment, an advantage, or the feeling of increased attention. All senses of the word trace back to the medieval Latin *interesse*, meaning "compensation for loss." And who isn't interested in getting paid?

ANSWER: C. A foundational statement for economics, this line in Smith's *Wealth of Nations* (1776) describes how a society in which each person pursues their own self-interest might come together as a harmonious whole.

"How much a dollar cost?"

 A Huckleberry Finn
....

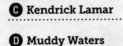 **B** Kanye West
....

C Kendrick Lamar
....

D Muddy Waters
....

SEE ALSO:

"Money often costs too much."
—RALPH WALDO EMERSON

ANSWER: C. Lamar's hit "How Much a Dollar Cost," a modern-day rap parable about the temptations of greed, was named by Barack Obama in 2015 as his favorite song of the year.

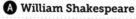
"The love of money is the root of all evil."

A William Shakespeare

B Paul the Apostle

C Moses

D Cicero

COUNTER POINT

"The lack of money is the root of all evil."

—MARK TWAIN
(popularized by)

ANSWER: B. This New Testament axiom has long been the subject of debate and reinterpretation. Later interpreters rendered the expression differently, such as Martin Luther, whose translation reads: "Avarice is a root of all evil."

"We are the best market; we are selling love."

A Steve Jobs

B Matt McMullen, inventor of world's first commercially viable sex robot

C Mother Teresa

D Hugh Hefner

FACT-CHECK

Finding love does not come cheap. In one survey, American singles estimated that, on average, they spend about $1,600 per year picking up tabs and paying for dating services. Who was it again who said, "Can't buy me love"?

ANSWER: C. Following a disastrous 1976 earthquake in Guatemala, Mother Teresa set up her charity center in an area that some residents said was needed for a street market. This was her response.

DIFFICULTY LEVEL

"We don't pay taxes. Only the little people pay taxes."

Ⓐ Imelda Marcos

Ⓑ Paris Hilton

Ⓒ Leona Helmsley

Ⓓ Bernie Madoff

DID YOU KNOW?

The scale of tax evasion is vast. An estimated $8.7 trillion is held in various tax shelters around the world. That's enough for every man, woman, and child on the planet to receive a $1,000 check.

ANSWER: C. Dubbed the "Queen of Mean" for her ruthless business style, Helmsley left her mark on New York City real estate with a string of luxury hotels. This infamous statement came out of a 1989 trial for tax evasion.

"God gave me my money."

A Sam Walton, founder of Walmart

B Robert Mugabe

C Charles Ponzi

D John D. Rockefeller

"It is easier for a camel to go through the eye of a needle than for a rich man to enter the kingdom of God"

—JESUS OF NAZARETH

ANSWER: D. The nineteenth-century tycoon amassed a fortune that would equal roughly $340 billion today. He once said of money: "You will find it the best of friends—if not the best friend—you have."

"All I do is satisfy a public demand."

A Larry Flynt

B Al Capone

C Mike Tyson

D Jenna Jameson

DID YOU KNOW?

As the cliché goes, the customer is always right—a dictum popularized by turn-of-the-century American retailers. Yet this level of customer service might seem skimpy compared to that of Japan, where the saying goes: "The customer is God."

ANSWER: B. Capone reportedly gave this as one of his regular answers to inquiries about his line of business—which, in point of fact, was bootlegging and organized crime. "Public service is my motto," he went on to say.

"What do you do when your competitor is drowning? Get a live hose and stick it in his mouth."

A Bill Gates

B Michael Phelps

C Tiger Woods

D Ray Kroc, creator of the McDonald's franchise

COUNTERPOINT "The competitor to be feared is one who never bothers about you at all, but goes on making his own business better all the time."

—HENRY FORD

ANSWER: D. Few restaurants succeed in the long run, let alone achieve the iconic status that McDonald's reached under the direction of Kroc, who took over the company when it was just a small-time regional burger chain.

"Money doesn't make you happy. I now have \$50 million but I was just as happy when I had \$48 million."

A Kim Kardashian

B Howard Hughes

C Arnold Schwarzenegger

D Mick Jagger

COUNTER POINT "People say that money is not the key to happiness, but I always figured if you have enough money, you can have a key made." —JOAN RIVERS

ANSWER: C. The *Terminator* star and former governor of California has only seen his wealth grow—if not his happiness—since he made this observation. He is now estimated to be worth some \$300 million.

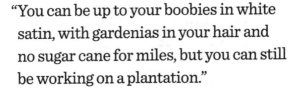
"You can be up to your boobies in white satin, with gardenias in your hair and no sugar cane for miles, but you can still be working on a plantation."

A Coretta Scott King

B Harriet Tubman

C Alice Walker

D Billie Holiday

DID YOU KNOW?

Even after slavery was abolished in the United States, many formerly enslaved people remained tied to the land due to the institution of sharecropping, in which farmers were forced to hand over part of their crop to landowners, leading to widespread indebtedness.

ANSWER: D. The one-of-a-kind jazz singer recorded this statement in her memoir *Lady Sings the Blues.* "I'm always making a comeback," Lady Day wrote, "but nobody ever tells me where I've been."

"The chief business of the American people is business."

A Milton Friedman

B Andrew Carnegie

C Calvin Coolidge

D John Kenneth Galbraith

DID YOU KNOW?

When Frenchman Alexis de Tocqueville visited America in the 1830s, he was immediately struck by Americans' mania for business. Wrote Tocqueville: "I know of no country, indeed, where the love of money has taken stronger hold on the affections of men."

ANSWER: C. Nicknamed "Silent Cal," Coolidge was a man of few words. When writer Dorothy Parker was informed in 1933 that the ex-president had passed away, she reportedly quipped: "How can they tell?"

"I'm not interested in making money. It's just that with my talent, I'm cursed with it."

A Noel Gallagher, of the rock band Oasis

....

B Naomi Campbell

....

C Cristiano Ronaldo

....

D Miles Davis

....

WORD UP 🖋

Incidentally, *talent* derives from an ancient Greek word that had to do with balance and weights— and thus money. In Homeric times, one talent could buy a single ox. In the New Testament, it was the highest denomination around.

ANSWER: A. This is how the notoriously lippy Oasis lead guitarist and songwriter once answered a query into his business acumen. "I'm a sh*t businessman," he averred.

"In this country, you gotta make the money first. Then when you get the money, you get the power. Then when you get the power, then you get the women."

A Tony Montana (*Scarface*)

B Charlie Sheen

C Joseph P. Kennedy Sr.

D Vito Corleone (*The Godfather*)

"The trouble with the rat race is that even if you win, you're still a rat."

—LILY TOMLIN (popularized by)

ANSWER: A. Brought to life in an unforgettable performance by Al Pacino, the fictional Cuban refugee-turned-drug-lord has become an enduring symbol of the American Dream—well, at least one version of it.

"Consider the lilies, how they grow—they neither toil nor spin."

 A Gautama Buddha

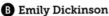 **B** Emily Dickinson

 C Jesus of Nazareth

 D Claude Monet

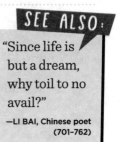

SEE ALSO:

"Since life is but a dream, why toil to no avail?"

—LI BAI, Chinese poet (701–762)

ANSWER: C. In his Sermon on the Mount, Jesus implores his flock not to worry about feeding or clothing themselves. Although the lilies don't so much as lift a finger, "even Solomon in all his glory was not arrayed like one of these."

"A woman must have money and a room of her own if she is to write fiction."

 A Harper Lee

 B Virginia Woolf

 C Zadie Smith

 D Percy Bysshe Shelley

SEE ALSO:

"Fiction writing is great. You can make up almost anything!"

—IVANA TRUMP

ANSWER: B. A touchstone of feminist literary theory, Woolf's essay "A Room of One's Own" posited that space must be made for women in the male-dominated literary tradition. "Anon, who wrote so many poems without signing them, was often a woman," Woolf wrote.

"Writing for a penny a word is ridiculous. If a man really wanted to make a million dollars, the best way to do it would be to start his own religion."

A Mary Baker Eddy

B William James

C Charles Dickens

D L. Ron Hubbard, founder of Scientology

 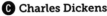

COUNTER POINT "I am a Millionaire. That is my religion."

—ANDREW UNDERSHAFT
(from George Bernard Shaw's *Major Barbara*)

ANSWER: D. In the late 1940s, Hubbard regularly professed that religion was the way to riches. The erstwhile sci-fi writer would soon publish *Dianetics: The Modern Science of Mental Health*, launching the religion of Scientology.

"No one in this world, so far as I know...
has ever lost money by underestimating
the intelligence of the great masses of
the plain people."

A P. T. Barnum

B William Jennings Bryan

C H. L. Mencken

D Rupert Murdoch

FACT-CHECK

To be fair, the same could be said of the
rich, as some of the biggest scams in
history have focused on separating the
wealthy from their money. Exhibit A: Bernie Madoff,
whose $65 billion Ponzi scheme defrauded everyone
from Kevin Bacon to Elie Wiesel.

ANSWER: C. The critic earned the title "American Nietzsche" for his sharp, if
cynical, takes on American life. This line is often misquoted as "No one ever
went broke underestimating the intelligence of the American people."

"Greed, for lack of a better word, is good. Greed is right, greed works."

A Gordon Gekko (*Wall Street*)

B Cornelius Vanderbilt

C Sheryl Sandberg

D Jordan Belfort,
aka the Wolf of Wall Street

SEE ALSO:

"Be fearful when others are greedy and greedy when others are fearful."

—WARREN BUFFETT

ANSWER: A. Played memorably by Michael Douglas in Oliver Stone's 1987 film *Wall Street*, Gekko saw greed in mystical terms: "Greed for life, for money, for love, knowledge has marked the upward surge of mankind."

"I pride myself on the fact that my work has no socially redeeming value."

 A Madonna

 B Gene Simmons

C John Waters

D Trey Parker, co-creator of *South Park*

SEE ALSO:

"If you have a message, call Western Union."

—MOSS HART, US playwright

ANSWER: C. Nicknamed the Pope of Trash, Waters pioneered a new style of transgressive camp in filmmaking. He wrote: "If someone vomits watching one of my films, it's like getting a standing ovation."

"Being a good boss means hiring talented people and then getting out of their way."

A Tina Fey

B Jack Welch

C Ted Turner

D Jeff Bezos

FACT-CHECK

Nobody likes to be micromanaged, but in some cases hands-off bosses might be even worse. Recent research from Harvard Business School found that more hands-on startup leaders are likelier to see their companies take off.

ANSWER: A. In her role as Liz Lemon in *30 Rock*, Fey often suffered the whims of a capricious network executive, played by Alec Baldwin. In reality, however, Fey was the true boss of *30 Rock*, serving as its showrunner.

"It is difficult to get a man to understand something, when his salary depends upon his not understanding it."

 A Upton Sinclair

 B Ralph Nader

 C Erin Brockovich

 D Alexander Hamilton

SEE ALSO:

"Few men have virtue to withstand the highest bidder."
—GEORGE WASHINGTON

ANSWER: A. Best known for his 1906 novel *The Jungle*, Sinclair also attempted a political career. That's how he learned this lesson, according to his memoir, *I, Candidate for Governor: And How I Got Licked.*

"Cash rules everything around me."

A Horace

B Walt Whitman

C Wu-Tang Clan

D Pablo Escobar

SEE ALSO:

"Cash. I just am not happy when I don't have it."

—ANDY WARHOL

ANSWER: C. This hip-hop axiom formed the basis of the Wu-Tang's 1994 hit "C.R.E.A.M." One of the group's most iconic songs, it was originally titled "Lifestyles of the Mega-Rich."

WORK & MONEY

129

"The workers have nothing to lose but their chains. They have a world to win. Workers of all countries, unite!"

 A Thomas Paine

B Thomas Jefferson

C Rosa Luxemburg

  D Karl Marx and Friedrich Engels

WORD UP

The English word *worker* is, unsurprisingly, quite old. But the notion of the worker as someone employed for a *wage* is of relatively recent vintage, springing up only in the mid-1800s.

ANSWER: D. The revolutionaries concluded their 1848 *Communist Manifesto* with these thundering sentences. It's hard to imagine that four years earlier, at the outset of their partnership, Marx and Engels were just a couple of twenty-something philosophers on a weeklong beer bender.

"Work is the curse of the drinking classes."

A Tallulah Bankhead

B Charles Bukowski

C Homer Simpson

D Oscar Wilde

FACT-CHECK

Who drinks more, rich or poor? Turns out there's no easy answer. Higher-status men are the most likely to be drinkers, a worldwide study recently found. Yet it's less well-off men—and high-status women—who engage the most in binge drinking.

ANSWER: D. Wilde achieved literary stardom thanks to his inexhaustible supply of quips and *mots*. Yet he spent the final years of his life penniless in Paris, thanks to years of persecution under English anti-homosexuality laws.

REVERSO!

"Ti esrever dna
ti pilf nwod gniht
ym tup."

—MISSY ELLIOTT

John Lennon said only one of these quotes. But which is it?

A "We thought we'd be really big in Liverpool."

B "We're more popular than Jesus now."

C "Everything is okay in the end. If it's not okay, it's not the end."

D "There was no play on words, we just didn't know how to spell the word 'beetle.'"

ANSWER: B. Lennon's "bigger-than-Jesus" comments in 1966 sparked outrage in America, leading to boycotts and death threats. Lennon would remain controversial until his untimely 1980 death. "If there's such a thing as genius, I am one," he once said. "And if there isn't, I don't care."

Marie Antoinette said only one of these quotes.
But which is it?

A "What they call a revolution is nothing more than a silly parade."

B "Let them eat cake!"

C "We had a beautiful dream and that was all."

D "In times of national distress, it is imperative not to lose one's head."

ANSWER: C. Among the many myths that have sprung up around Marie Antoinette was her apocryphal retort when told the commoners had no bread to eat; there is no evidence that "Let them eat cake" ever passed Marie Antoinette's lips. Her "beautiful dream" line came in response to entreaties that she attempt to escape her imprisonment after the French Revolution, which she steadfastly refused to do without her children.

Sigmund Freud did NOT say one of these quotes. Which is the fake?

 A "The interpretation of dreams is the royal road to a knowledge of the unconscious activities of the mind."

B "Sometimes a cigar is just a cigar."

C "At bottom God is nothing other than an exalted father."

D "The sexual life of adult women is a 'dark continent' for psychology."

ANSWER: B. Often pictured with a cigar, the grandfather of psychoanalysis might well have been aware of the psychosexual connotations of his smoking habit. But scholars believe this quip was a fabrication.

Andy Warhol did NOT say one of these quotes. Which is the fake?

A "The secret to my success is that it's far easier to paint the tomato can than the tomato."

B "If you want to know all about Andy Warhol, just look at the surface of my paintings and films and me, and there I am. There's nothing behind it."

C "Sex is the biggest nothing of all time."

D "Being good in business is the most fascinating kind of art. Making money is art and working is art and good business is the best art."

ANSWER: A. Warhol didn't make this remark, but he did once explain his interest in painting Campbell's tomato soup thusly: "I used to drink it, I used to have the same lunch every day, for twenty years." Go figure.

Rosa Parks said only one of these quotes.
But which is it?

A "The only tired I was, was tired of giving in."

B "Power is not given to you. You have to take it."

C "Sometimes taking a stand means taking a seat."

D "Life's most persistent and urgent question is: 'What are you doing for others?'"

ANSWER: A. In the typical telling of the Rosa Parks story, the 42-year-old seamstress is depicted as tired out after a long day of work. But as Parks would later write in her memoir, she was a *different* kind of tired.

Mahatma Gandhi said only one of these quotes. But which is it?

A "First they ignore you. Then they laugh at you. Then they attack you. Then you win."

B "If you're going to be a bear, be a grizzly."

C "It is unwise to be too sure of one's own wisdom."

D "An eye for an eye will make the whole world blind."

ANSWER: C. Gandhi has long been a magnet for dubious quotations. Perhaps the wittiest line attributed to him may be apocryphal; scholars have yet to confirm that, when asked his thoughts on Western civilization, Gandhi replied, "I think it would be a good idea."

DIFFICULTY LEVEL

Paris Hilton did NOT say one of these quotes. Which is the fake?

A "I think every decade has an iconic blonde—like Marilyn Monroe or Princess Diana—and right now, I'm that icon."

B "That's hot."

C "Every woman should have four pets in her life. A mink in her closet, a jaguar in her garage, a tiger in her bed, and a jackass who pays for everything."

D "The only rule is don't be boring. Dress cute wherever you go. Life is too short to blend in."

ANSWER: C. As much as this widely misattributed quotation fits the Paris Hilton brand, the quip long predates the reality-TV star and heiress to the Hilton hotel fortune.

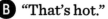

Stephen King said only one of these quotes.
But which is it?

A "There is no such thing as a moral or an immoral book. Books are well written or badly written."

B "The most merciful thing in the world, I think, is the inability of the human mind to correlate all its contents."

C "Nothing in life is to be feared, it is only to be understood."

D "I'm a salami writer. I try to write good salami, but salami is salami."

ANSWER: D. Despite being one of the most successful scribblers of all time—with an estimated 350 million books sold—King has managed to keep a sense of humor about his prolific talent.

Eva Perón did NOT say one of these quotes. Which is the fake?

A "Without fanaticism one cannot accomplish anything."

B "When I die, take off the red [nail] varnish and replace it with a plain varnish."

C "Don't cry for me, Argentina."

D "Never abandon the poor—they are the only ones who know how to be loyal."

ANSWER: C. Though this lyric is imprinted in the minds of English-speaking audiences thanks to the Andrew Lloyd Webber musical *Evita* and its film adaptation starring Madonna, the real Eva Perón—actress and wife of the authoritarian president Juan Perón—never actually said this.

Oprah Winfrey said only one of these quotes.
But which is it?

A "If you stop being better, you stop being good."

B "The power of positive thinking may work a tad better when you have a billion dollars."

C "Words build bridges into unexplored regions."

D "My idea of heaven is a great big baked potato and someone to share it with."

ANSWER: D. This is what Winfrey told *People* magazine back in 1985, as her fame was just starting to take off. Who knows if her dreams of the afterlife have changed since becoming a billionaire.

DIFFICULTY LEVEL

Adolf Hitler said only one of these quotes.
But which is it?

A "The best way to take control over a people and control them utterly is to take a little of their freedom at a time."

B "I am intimidated by the fear of being average."

C "If you repeat a lie often enough, it becomes the truth."

D "I go the way that Providence dictates with the assurance of a sleepwalker."

ANSWER: D. Hitler delivered this line in a speech in Munich in 1936, just a few weeks before a purported "election" delivered his party a 99 percent mandate to continue its aggressive military policies.

Vincent van Gogh said only one of these quotes.
But which is it?

A "I became insane, with long intervals of horrible sanity."

B "I cannot help it that my paintings do not sell. The time will come when people will see that they are worth more than the price of the paint."

C "I would rather die of passion than of boredom."

D "[Paul] Gauguin asked me to lend him an ear. So I complied."

ANSWER: B. In an 1888 missive to his brother Theo, Van Gogh keenly anticipated his own coming celebrity, which had started to emerge in his final years but really took off only decades later—especially at the publication of his deeply passionate letters.

Elizabeth Taylor did NOT say one of these quotes. Which is the fake?

A "A woman has got to love a bad man once or twice in her life, to be thankful for a good one."

B "There is no deodorant like success."

C "When people say, 'she's got everything,' I've only one answer: I haven't had tomorrow."

D "Some of my best leading men have been dogs and horses."

ANSWER: A. Having married eight times in her life, including twice with fellow film giant Richard Burton, Taylor might have had some expertise in this department. But this sometimes-misattributed quote originated instead with novelist Marjorie Rawlings.

Georgia O'Keeffe did NOT say one of these quotes. Which is the fake?

A "One doesn't see a thing, then paint it. Seeing comes after."

B "I hate flowers—I paint them because they're cheaper than models and they don't move."

C "That Blue [of the sky] that will always be there as it is now after all man's destruction is finished."

D "Since I cannot sing, I paint."

ANSWER: A. In a career spanning five-plus decades, the "Mother of American Modernism" did maintain some highfalutin ideas about art and painting. But this wasn't one of them.

Ayn Rand said only one of these quotes. But which is it?

A "To be free, a man must be free of his brothers."

B "I can summarize my philosophy thusly: looking out for number one."

C "The question isn't who is going to let me, it's who is going to stop me?"

D "Freedom is always and exclusively freedom for the one who thinks differently."

ANSWER: A. The author of books including *Atlas Shrugged* and *The Fountainhead*, Rand was one of the most influential conservative writers of the twentieth century. She devised the philosophical system known as objectivism, whose central tenet is overriding self-interest.

Winston Churchill said only one of these quotes. But which is it?

A "There is nothing new in the world except the history you do not know."

B "The Americans can always be trusted to do the right thing, once all other possibilities have been exhausted."

C "If you're going through hell, keep going."

D "We are all worms, but I do believe I am a glow-worm."

ANSWER: D. The prolific wordsmith, who published a staggering 72 volumes when not serving at 10 Downing Street, reportedly delivered this mordant observation at a dinner party after bemoaning the inexorable passage of time. He had just turned 32.

POLITICS
& WAR

"Politics is
war without
bloodshed."

—MAO ZEDONG

"Politics is the art of the possible."

A Archduke Franz Ferdinand

B Otto von Bismarck

C Neville Chamberlain

D John Adams

COUNTER POINT

"The art of politics is smiling when you feel like you're swallowing a turd." —BILL CLINTON

ANSWER: B. Bismarck, whose diplomatic maneuverings and military adventures led to the creation of the modern German state, is remembered as one of the most skilled statesmen in history.

"Those who would give up essential liberty, to purchase a little temporary safety, deserve neither liberty nor safety."

A Dorothy Day

B John Locke

C Woodrow Wilson

D Benjamin Franklin

SEE ALSO:

"I would rather be exposed to the inconveniences attending too much liberty, than those attending too small a degree of it."

—THOMAS JEFFERSON

ANSWER: D. This catchy maxim has had several afterlives, particularly among civil libertarians protesting perceived encroachments on speech. Yet in its original context, Franklin's quote had more to do with taxation than speech.

3
DIFFICULTY LEVEL

"It is true that liberty is precious—so precious that it must be rationed."

 A Andrew Jackson

 B President Coriolanus Snow
(*The Hunger Games*)

C George Orwell

D Vladimir Ilyich Lenin

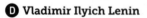

SEE ALSO:

"O liberty! what crimes are committed in thy name!"

—MADAME ROLAND,
French revolutionary

ANSWER: D. This quotation has come to epitomize the hard-nosed realpolitik of Leninism. Reportedly, Lenin's definition of political science was: "Who masters whom?"

"I am not truly free if I am taking away someone else's freedom, just as surely as I am not free when my freedom is taken away from me. The oppressed and the oppressor alike are robbed of their humanity."

A Medgar Evers

B Henry David Thoreau

C Nelson Mandela

D Edmund Burke

DID YOU KNOW?

In the infamous Stanford Prison Experiment, students were randomly assigned to role-play as either guards or prisoners. After the guards got a little *too* into their roles, the study was terminated just six days in.

ANSWER: C. Mandela achieved international fame for his decades-long struggle to undo the South African system of racial apartheid—a cause for which he spent more than a third of his adult life in prison.

"I am most anxious to enlist everyone who can speak or write to join in checking this mad, wicked folly of 'Women's Rights,' with all its attendant horrors."

A Betsy Ross

B Theodore Roosevelt

C Queen Victoria

D Phyllis Schlafly

WORD UP

The first English language book on women's rights, *The Law's Resolutions of Women's Rights*, was published in 1632. Yet it was hardly an enlightened document; chapter titles include: "That which the wife hath is the husband's" and "The baron may beat his wife."

ANSWER: C. Victoria may have been a popular queen, but she was no feminist hero. Elsewhere in the 1870 letter that contains this quotation, she writes: "Feminists ought to get a good whipping."

"Democracy is the worst form of government except all those other forms that have been tried from time to time."

 A Franz Kafka

B Franklin D. Roosevelt

C Winston Churchill

D Leon Trotsky

COUNTER POINT

"Democracy! Bah! When I hear that word I reach for my feather boa!"

—ALLEN GINSBERG

Answer: C. Churchill was the face of British resolve amidst the carnage of World War II, during which Nazi Germany dropped more than 40,000 tons of bombs on England. As he declared in 1940: "We shall never surrender."

"The one thing that doesn't abide by majority rule is a person's conscience."

A Atticus Finch
(*To Kill a Mockingbird*)

B Benedict Arnold

C Jane Fonda

D Julius Rosenberg

DID YOU KNOW?

The Founding Fathers weren't unabashed champions of majority rule. James Madison warned that under the majority, "the rights of the minor party become insecure." Democracy could "degenerate into an anarchy," wrote John Adams.

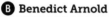

ANSWER: A. Though Finch is the hero of Harper Lee's first novel, his saintly image was dashed 55 years later with the publication of Lee's *Go Set a Watchman*, in which he becomes a defender of segregation.

"Extremism in the defense of liberty is no vice. Moderation in the pursuit of justice is no virtue."

A Emiliano Zapata

B Samuel Adams

C Timothy McVeigh

D Barry Goldwater

SEE ALSO:

"The question is not whether we will be extremists, but what kind of extremists we will be."

—MARTIN LUTHER KING JR.

ANSWER: D. Though the Arizona senator and 1964 Republican candidate for president lost in a landslide, his campaign helped fuel a resurgence of American conservatism.

DIFFICULTY LEVEL

"All men would be tyrants if they could."

A Benito Mussolini

B Aristotle

C Abigail Adams

D Dennis the Menace

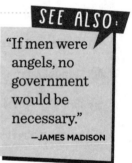

SEE ALSO:

"If men were angels, no government would be necessary."

—JAMES MADISON

ANSWER: C. Often, the word "men" means all humankind. Not so here. In a 1776 letter, Adams beseeched husband John Adams to "Remember the Ladies" in forming the new nation: "If perticuliar care & attention is not paid to the Ladies we are determined to foment a Rebellion," she wrote.

"Speak softly and carry a big stick; you will go far."

A Ulysses S. Grant

B Sun Tzu

C Theodore Roosevelt

D Fred Rogers

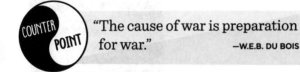

COUNTER POINT

"The cause of war is preparation for war."

—W.E.B. DU BOIS

ANSWER: C. This was the summation of Roosevelt's diplomatic philosophy, which emphasized discretion combined with overwhelming firepower. Roosevelt said he appropriated the saying from a West African proverb.

"You can no more win a war than you can win an earthquake."

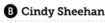 **A** Jeannette Rankin, first woman in the US Congress

 **B** Cindy Sheehan

 C Noam Chomsky

D Dwight D. Eisenhower

DID YOU KNOW?

Yeah, but what if you could win a war *with* an earthquake? This was the thought behind several secret military programs, both rumored and confirmed. The World War II-era Project Seal in New Zealand, for instance, aimed to create a weaponized tsunami.

ANSWER: A. First elected to the House of Representatives in 1916—before women nationwide had the right to vote—Rankin later became the only Member of Congress to vote against US entry into World War II.

DIFFICULTY LEVEL

"Gentlemen, you can't fight in here! This is the War Room!"

A Donald Rumsfeld

B Robert McNamara

C President Merkin Muffley (*Dr. Strangelove*)

D Nikita Khrushchev

DID YOU KNOW?

The earliest American version of a war room was Abraham Lincoln's telegraph office, next door to the White House. The office manager later wrote that during the Civil War, Lincoln spent more time there than anywhere outside of the White House.

ANSWER: C. This is the signature line, spoken by actor Peter Sellers, from Stanley Kubrick's 1964 antiwar farce—full title *Dr. Strangelove or: How I Learned to Stop Worrying and Love the Bomb.*

"The only thing that's been a worse flop than the organization of nonviolence has been the organization of violence."

Ⓐ Joan Baez

Ⓑ Mikhail Gorbachev

Ⓒ Martin Luther King Jr.

Ⓓ Yoko Ono

DID YOU KNOW?

The modern American concept of nonviolence has its roots in the abolition struggle, specifically the prolific anti-slavery advocate William Lloyd Garrison. Garrison stressed "moral suasion" over force.

ANSWER: A. Baez helped bring folk music mainstream and played a key role in getting Bob Dylan's career off the ground. She penned this line in her 1968 memoir *Daybreak*.

"The Pope? How many divisions has he got?"

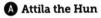

A Attila the Hun

B Adolf Hitler

C Joseph Stalin

D General Curtis LeMay

DID YOU KNOW?

The Pope may not command armies, but there is the Papal Swiss Guard, a 500-year-old corps of Swiss natives decked out in colorful Renaissance-era stripes and shiny armor.

ANSWER: C. This is how Stalin is said to have responded when a French diplomat encouraged him to promote Catholicism in the Soviet Union in order to please the Pope. Needless to say, Uncle Joe was not amused.

"I came, I saw, I conquered."

A Napoleon Bonaparte

B Alexander the Great

C Superman

D Julius Caesar

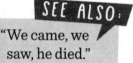

SEE ALSO:

"We came, we saw, he died."

—HILLARY CLINTON,
on Muammar Gaddafi

ANSWER: D. This famous boast (Latin: *Veni, vidi, vici*) didn't follow some world-historic triumph, like, say, defeating Gaul. Instead, Caesar purportedly said it after the relatively minor Battle of Zela, in modern-day Turkey.

"Pray for the dead and fight like hell for the living!"

A Eleanor Roosevelt

B Douglas MacArthur

C Robert E. Lee

D Mary Harris "Mother" Jones

 DID YOU KNOW?

During the twentieth century, at least 108 million people were killed in wars and other conflicts. That's a lot of prayer!

ANSWER: D. The matriarch of the American labor movement, Mother Jones took part in many bitter early twentieth-century labor struggles, including the Battle of Blair Mountain, in which dozens of protesters were killed.

DIFFICULTY LEVEL

"The tree of liberty must be refreshed from time to time with the blood of patriots and tyrants. It is its natural manure."

A Ho Chi Minh

B George Washington

C Thomas Jefferson

D Nat Turner

SEE ALSO:

"Those who make peaceful revolution impossible will make violent revolution inevitable."

—JOHN F. KENNEDY

ANSWER: C. This was the future president's reaction in 1787 to news of an attempted insurrection in Massachusetts. Elsewhere, Jefferson added: "A little rebellion now and then is a good thing."

"History is made by active, determined minorities, not by the majority, which seldom has a clear and consistent idea of what it really wants."

A Margaret Mead

B Theodore Kaczynski, aka the Unabomber

C Susan B. Anthony

D Maximilien Robespierre

DID YOU KNOW?

According to a recent study, once a pressure group reaches a critical mass of 25 percent, it can sway the entire population. Now if only we could get a quarter of the population to agree that weekends include Fridays . . .

ANSWER: B. This line occurs in the Unabomber's infamous manifesto. Kaczynski's brother read it in the newspaper, recognized his older sibling's writing style, and tipped off the FBI, leading to Ted's arrest.

"When a great many people are unable to find work, unemployment results."

A George W. Bush

B Al Gore

C Donald Trump

D Calvin Coolidge

 **FACT-CHECK** True.

ANSWER: D. Silent Cal, never one for fancy wordplay, couldn't have been more direct than in this famed understatement, attributed to him by longtime *New York Herald-Tribune* editor Stanley Walker.

"I am not a member of any organized party—I am a Democrat."

A James Carville

B Will Rogers

C John F. Kennedy

D Bernie Sanders

WORD UP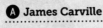

The Democratic party was founded in the late 1700s by followers of Thomas Jefferson and James Madison, who went under the banner Democratic-Republicans. Depending on your definition, the US Democratic party constitutes the oldest continuous political party in the world.

ANSWER: B. Rogers, a cowboy turned comedian, brought a unique blend of homespun wisdom and western charm to his movies, vaudeville routines, and more than 3,600 syndicated newspaper columns.

"I will not make age an issue of this campaign. I am not going to exploit for political purposes my opponent's youth and inexperience."

Ⓐ Mahathir Mohamad, world's oldest elected leader

Ⓑ Richard Nixon

Ⓒ Ronald Reagan

Ⓓ William McKinley

DID YOU KNOW?

The oldest-ever US election, in terms of ages of the major parties' candidates, was that of 2016. Hillary Clinton and Donald Trump had a combined 139 years between them on election day.

ANSWER: C. This statement came during a 1984 presidential debate with Democratic challenger Walter Mondale. Reagan would be diagnosed with Alzheimer's five years after leaving office.

"Polls are for strippers and cross-country skiers."

A Ross Perot

B Huey Long

C Stephen Bannon

D Sarah Palin

> ### SEE ALSO:
>
> "I wonder how far Moses would have gone if he'd taken a poll in Egypt. What would Jesus Christ have preached if he'd taken a poll in Israel?"
>
> —**HARRY S. TRUMAN**

ANSWER: D. The Alaskan vice-presidential-candidate-turned-reality-TV-star delivered this line during a 2011 speech.

"In the United States today, we have more than our share of the nattering nabobs of negativism."

A Spiro Agnew

B Malcolm X

C Bob Dole

D Nancy Reagan

WORD UP

Nabob originally referred to a deputy governor in India's Mughal Empire. The term later attached to British colonialists returning from India, and by extension came to mean anyone of great wealth, political import, or excessively high status.

ANSWER: A. Richard Nixon's first vice president Spiro Agnew launched this dig at the press, yet its speechwriter William Safire, who went on to have a successful career as a columnist, deserves credit.

"I could stand in the middle of Fifth Avenue and shoot somebody and I wouldn't lose any voters."

A William "Boss" Tweed

B Fiorello La Guardia

C Frank Underwood
(*House of Cards*)

D Donald Trump

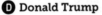

SEE ALSO:

"Hell, I never vote *for* anybody. I always vote *against*."

—W. C. FIELDS

ANSWER: D. The 45th president of the United States did actually say this while campaigning in 2016. Needless to say, it was not empirically tested.

"I remain just one thing, and one thing only—and that is a clown. It places me on a far higher plane than any politician."

A Jon Stewart

B Silvio Berlusconi

C Charlie Chaplin

D Stephen Colbert

SEE ALSO:

"A politician is an arse upon which everyone has sat except a man."

—E. E. CUMMINGS

ANSWER: C. The silent-era comedy legend ventured into the world of sound for the first time with his 1940 film *The Great Dictator*. Chaplin's caricature of a Hitler-like tyrant made the movie his most explicitly political.

"If anything is certain, it is that I myself am not a Marxist."

A Barack Obama

B Karl Marx

C Vladimir Putin

D Groucho Marx

SEE ALSO:

> "*Isms*, in my opinion, are not good. A person should not believe in an *ism*, he should believe in himself."
>
> —FERRIS BUELLER

ANSWER: B. This statement, recalled by Marx's longtime colleague Friedrich Engels, may come as a surprise, but Marx felt uneasy about a monolithic version of his varied thoughts.

"When they go low, we go high."

A Michelle Obama

B Charles de Gaulle

C Melania Trump

D Josiah Bartlet (*The West Wing*)

COUNTER POINT

"War has rules. Mud-wrestling has rules. Politics has no rules."

—ROSS PEROT

ANSWER: A. The former first lady's message to America during the caustic 2016 presidential election was meant to inspire a renewed attention to civility in the political discourse. Well, it was a valiant effort, at least.

"When the president does it, that means it is not illegal."

Ⓐ Franklin D. Roosevelt

Ⓑ Richard Nixon

Ⓒ Rudy Giuliani

Ⓓ Abraham Lincoln

SEE ALSO:

"The illegal we do immediately, the unconstitutional takes a little longer."

—HENRY KISSINGER

ANSWER: B. "Tricky Dick" made this remark to journalist David Frost three years after resigning from the White House. "I gave them a sword," Nixon said of his downfall. "And they stuck it in and they twisted it with relish."

"If one morning I walked on top of the water across the Potomac River, the headline that afternoon would read: 'President Can't Swim.'"

Ⓐ Bill Clinton

Ⓑ Barack Obama

Ⓒ Herbert Hoover

Ⓓ Lyndon B. Johnson

SEE ALSO:

"[Journalists] are a sort of assassins who sit with loaded blunderbusses at the corner of streets and fire them off for hire or for sport at any passenger whom they select."

—JOHN QUINCY ADAMS

ANSWER: D. This quip epitomizes the typically fractious relationship between the press and the Oval Office. Elsewhere, Johnson gibed: "The fact that a man is a newspaper reporter is evidence of some flaw of character."

"All animals are equal, but some animals are more equal than others."

A Hobbes (*Calvin and Hobbes*)

B Niccolò Machiavelli

C George Orwell

D Ingrid Newkirk, cofounder of PETA

> **SEE ALSO:**
> "One citizen is equal to another, but perhaps this one is slightly more equal than the others."
> —SILVIO BERLUSCONI

ANSWER: C. In Orwell's political allegory *Animal Farm*, what begins as a livestock uprising against the farmers ends up elevating a class of traitorous pigs, who ally with the humans.

THE SCUTTLE-BUTT

"He could shake your hand and stab you in the back at the same time."

—HUNTER S. THOMPSON ON RICHARD NIXON

Former US cabinet member **Edwin M. Stanton** said the following. Who was he talking about?

"Now he belongs to the ages."

Ⓐ Robert F. Kennedy

Ⓑ Abraham Lincoln

Ⓒ George Washington

Ⓓ John F. Kennedy

ANSWER: B. Secretary of War Stanton reportedly made this remark upon Lincoln's death, the morning after the president was shot by John Wilkes Booth. Some versions, however, have it: "Now he belongs to the angels."

MINI-GAME: THE SCUTTLEBUTT

184

Pop star **Boy George** said the following. Who was he talking about?

"She's a gay man trapped in a woman's body."

A Margaret Thatcher

B Madonna

C Liza Minnelli

D Barbra Streisand

ANSWER: B. The pop giant has long been cherished as a gay icon. During a question-and-answer session on Reddit in 2013, she confirmed Boy George's suspicions, typing matter-of-factly: "I am a gay man."

MINI-GAME: THE SCUTTLEBUTT

185

Writer **Mary McCarthy** said the following. Who was she talking about?

"Every word she writes is a lie, including 'and' and 'the.'"

 A Nora Ephron

B Lillian Hellman

 C Susan Sontag

D Sylvia Plath

ANSWER: B. Hellman, a successful playwright, is famous for her declaration, "I cannot and will not cut my conscience to fit this year's fashions," in a letter to the House Un-American Activities Committee.

Writer and social critic **Gore Vidal** said the following. Who was he talking about?

"A genius with the IQ of a moron."

A Andy Warhol

B William F. Buckley

C Norman Mailer

D Andy Kaufman

ANSWER: A. There have been few modern artists as divisive as Warhol, who pioneered an unabashedly superficial style in his art and personal demeanor. Remarked Bianca Jagger: "I mistook his silences for intelligence."

Singer and actor **Bing Crosby** said the following. Who was he talking about?

"An average guy who could carry a tune."

A Wolfgang Amadeus Mozart

B Frank Sinatra

C Paul McCartney

D Bing Crosby

ANSWER: D. Crosby, who also had an Oscar-winning film career, reportedly suggested this line for his own epitaph.

MINI-GAME: THE SCUTTLEBUTT

188

Hollywood icon **Bette Davis** said the following. Who was she talking about?

"She has slept with every male star at MGM except Lassie."

A Marilyn Monroe

B Joan Crawford

C Judy Garland

D Grace Kelly

ANSWER: B. No Hollywood feud has produced such venom as the one between Crawford and Davis, who starred together in the 1962 classic *Whatever Happened to Baby Jane?*

MINI-GAME: THE SCUTTLEBUTT

189

Nobel Prize–winning novelist **Toni Morrison** said the following. Who was she talking about?

"This is our first black President."

A Bill Clinton

B Jesse Jackson

C Barack Obama

D Aretha Franklin

ANSWER: A. This was Morrison's conclusion amid the high-profile investigations into the president, which she saw as a kind of racially inflicted persecution.

MINI-GAME: THE SCUTTLEBUTT

190

Pop vocalist **Mariah Carey** said the following. Who was she talking about?

"I don't know her."

A Miley Cyrus

B Cleopatra

C Mother Teresa

D Jennifer Lopez

ANSWER: D. Asked about Lopez in an early-2000s interview, Carey gave this laconic response, which has since become a stock image in the online meme lexicon. The two pop divas' rivalry has lasted for nearly two decades.

MINI-GAME: THE SCUTTLEBUTT

191

Writer **Dorothy Parker** said the following. Who was she talking about?

"He has a capacity for enjoyment so vast that he gives away great chunks to those about him, and never even misses them. . . . He can take you to a bicycle race and make it raise your hair."

A Ted Williams

B Errol Flynn

C Ernest Hemingway

D Buster Keaton

ANSWER: C. This oft-cited passage comes from Parker's 1929 profile of Hemingway, which also popularized Hemingway's memorable definition of the word *guts*: "grace under pressure."

Aristocrat and novelist **Lady Caroline Lamb** said the following. Who was she talking about?

"Mad, bad, and dangerous to know."

 A Aleister Crowley

B Lord Byron

C Mary Shelley

D William Blake

ANSWER: B. This was the impression Byron made on Lamb, who remained infatuated with the flamboyant Romantic poet for years after their short tryst.

MINI-GAME: THE SCUTTLEBUTT
193

British journalist and essayist **Evelyn Waugh** said the following. Who was he talking about?

"Simply a radio personality who outlived his prime."

A Winston Churchill

B George Orwell

C H. G. Wells

D King George VI

ANSWER: A. This was Waugh's assessment of Churchill's death in 1965. The British statesman was more often seen on the other side of insults.

MINI-GAME: THE SCUTTLEBUTT

194

Venezuelan president **Hugo Chávez** said the following. Who was he talking about?

"Yesterday, the devil came here ... and it smells of sulfur still today, this table that I am now standing in front of."

 Tony Blair

B George W. Bush

C Bill Clinton

D Kofi Annan

ANSWER: B. The Venezuelan revolutionary, who ruled the South American country from 1999 until his death in 2013, relished ruffling American feathers with his fiery rhetoric. He referred to Bush as "Mr. Danger."

Former Pink Floyd bassist **Roger Waters** sang the following. Who was he talking about?

"Shine on you crazy diamond."

A Haile Selassie

B Neil Diamond

C Syd Barrett

D Jerry Hall

ANSWER: C. The original leader of the group during the 1960s, Barrett left due to struggles with mental health and drugs. He mysteriously reappeared one day in the studio during the sessions that produced the song about him.

An anonymous movie studio official said the following. Who were they talking about?

"Can't act. Slightly bald. Also dances."

A Gregory Hines

B Fred Astaire

C John Travolta

D Gene Kelly

ANSWER: B. Astaire owed his big break to dancing, yet he saw nothing special in his art. "I have no desire to prove anything by it," he once said. "I have never used it as an outlet or a means of expressing myself. I just dance."

Pop star and television personality Cher said the following. Who was she talking about?

"...the female equivalent of a counterfeit $20 bill. Half of what you see is a pretty good reproduction, the rest is a fraud."

Ⓐ Madonna

Ⓑ Cher

Ⓒ Lady Gaga

Ⓓ Carly Simon

ANSWER: B. Few stars have reinvented themselves more than Cher, who found success with husband Sonny Bono on television, the big screen, and as a solo artist.

Hollywood leading man **Humphrey Bogart** said the following. Who was he talking about?

"If he had lived, he'd never have been able to live up to his publicity."

A Rudolph Valentino

B Buddy Holly

C Benjamin "Bugsy" Siegel

D James Dean

ANSWER: D. Bogart offered this mordant observation after Dean died in a car crash in 1955 at the age of 24. The *Rebel Without a Cause* star "died at just the right time," Bogart said. "He left behind a legend."

MOTIVATION

"Kid, you'll move
mountains!"

—DR. SEUSS

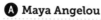

"Hope is the thing with feathers that perches in the soul."

A Maya Angelou

B Emily Dickinson

C Woodstock (*Peanuts*)

D Christina Rossetti

COUNTER POINT

"Hope is not 'the thing with feathers.' The thing with feathers has turned out to be my nephew. I must take him to a specialist in Zurich." —WOODY ALLEN

ANSWER: B. The reclusive nineteenth-century poet wrote roughly 1,800 poems while living a hermit's existence in Amherst, Massachusetts. Fewer than a dozen were actually published during her lifetime.

"Move fast and break things. Unless you are breaking stuff, you are not moving fast enough."

A Henry Ford

B Mark Zuckerberg

C Jeff Bezos

D Chuck Yeager, first pilot to break the sound barrier

SEE ALSO:

"A good plan violently executed *now* is better than a perfect plan next week."

—GEORGE S. PATTON

ANSWER: B. The Facebook founder made this the de facto motto of his fast-growing social network, plastering the walls of the company headquarters with posters bearing the message.

"You see things; and you say 'Why?' But I dream things that never were; and I say 'Why not?'"

A George Bernard Shaw

B Robert F. Kennedy

C Thomas Edison

D H. P. Lovecraft

DID YOU KNOW?

Some of history's biggest creative breakthroughs occurred in dreamland, such as the periodic table, the Beatles song "Yesterday," *The Strange Case of Dr. Jekyll and Mr. Hyde*, and Einstein's theory of relativity.

ANSWER: A. This quote is often misattributed to Bobby Kennedy, who paraphrased it often in speeches. But the line appears originally in Shaw's play *Back to Methuselah*.

"I have the same goal I've had since I was a girl. I want to rule the world."

A Madonna

B Oprah Winfrey

C Beyoncé

D Margaret Thatcher

SEE ALSO:

"At the age of six I wanted to be a cook. At seven I wanted to be Napoleon. And my ambition has been growing steadily ever since."

—SALVADOR DALÍ

ANSWER: A. Madonna did manage to rule the music world, at least. The _Guinness Book of World Records_ lists her as the most successful female recording artist in history, with more than 300 million records sold.

"The road to Easy Street goes through the sewer."

A Betty Ford

B Andy Dufresne (*The Shawshank Redemption*)

C Dean Martin

D John Madden

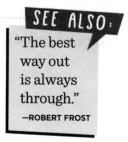

SEE ALSO:

"The best way out is always through."

—ROBERT FROST

ANSWER: D. The storied NFL coach-turned-announcer is known for using bluntly evocative language to describe the game of football. Another of his sayings: "Don't worry about the horse being blind, just load the wagon."

"Sometimes I've believed as many as six impossible things before breakfast."

A M. C. Escher

B Pablo Picasso

C White Queen (*Through the Looking-Glass*)

D John Harvey Kellogg

COUNTER POINT

"'It is not possible'...that is not French." —NAPOLEON BONAPARTE

ANSWER: C. Lewis Carroll, author of the revered Alice in Wonderland series, believed children's literature should reflect the boundless imagination of youth. "Every child has a world of his own," he wrote.

"A journey of a thousand miles starts with a single step."

A Neil Armstrong

B Lao Tzu

C Dale Carnegie

D Ovid

"Do not put off until tomorrow what can be put off till day-after-tomorrow just as well."

—MARK TWAIN

ANSWER: B. This is the common English rendering of an expression from the *Tao Te Ching*, which, translated literally, reads "The journey of a thousand // starts from where one stands." // Is actually about a third of a mile.

"Courage is the price that life exacts for granting peace."

A Amelia Earhart

B Alexandre Dumas

C Rosa Parks

D Jacques Cousteau

SEE ALSO:

"Life shrinks or expands according to one's courage."

—ANAÏS NIN

ANSWER: A. The fearless navigator was an amateur poet as well. The poem that contains this quote goes on: "The soul that knows it not, knows no release from little things."

DIFFICULTY LEVEL

"I want to put a ding in the universe."

A Sally Ride

B Robert Heinlein

C Steve Jobs

D J. Robert Oppenheimer

DID YOU KNOW?

Though it may concern those of us who enjoy Earth's continued existence, scientists believe it's possible for modern particle colliders to produce microscopic black holes. Thankfully, however, these quantum-scale black holes pose no apparent danger.

ANSWER: C. The late cofounder of Apple has become something of a patron saint in Silicon Valley for his ingenuity and business savvy. Another of Jobs's expressions: "It's more fun to be a pirate than to join the Navy."

"Seize the day, put no trust in the future."

A Robin Williams

B Julius Caesar

C Alexander Pope

D Horace

COUNTER POINT

"The best way to predict the future is to invent it." —ALAN KAY

ANSWER: D. Also known by its original Latin—*carpe diem*—this inspirational dictum appeared in Horace's *Odes*, published in 23 BCE. The saying also made a cameo in the film *Dead Poets Society*, starring Robin Williams.

DIFFICULTY LEVEL

"I have to dream and reach for the stars, and if I miss a star then I grab a handful of clouds."

A Kanye West

B Judy Garland

C Mike Tyson

D Peter Pan

SEE ALSO:

"To infinity and beyond!"

—BUZZ LIGHTYEAR
(Toy Story)

ANSWER: C. The troubled heavyweight champion boxer, who infamously bit rival Evander Holyfield's ears during a title bout, has always proved a lively and unpredictable interview subject.

"One can never consent to creep when one feels an impulse to soar."

A Orville Wright

B Helen Keller

C Buzz Aldrin

D Harry Potter

SEE ALSO:

"You just think lovely wonderful thoughts, and they lift you up in the air."

—PETER PAN, on how to fly

ANSWER: B. Rendered deaf and blind by a childhood illness, Keller learned to communicate with the help of teacher Anne Sullivan. After her accomplishments were publicized, she became an international icon.

"I'll tell you what freedom means to me: no fear."

A Nina Simone

B Bobby Sands

C Captain America

D Toni Morrison

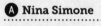

SEE ALSO

"We look forward to a world founded upon four essential freedoms . . . the fourth is freedom from fear."

—FRANKLIN D. ROOSEVELT

ANSWER: A. One of the most singular voices in jazz, Simone risked her career to speak out on the political issues of her time. Simone's 1964 "Mississippi Goddam" became an anthem among activists.

"What does not kill me makes me stronger."

Ⓐ Margaret Fuller

....

Ⓑ Count Dracula

....

Ⓒ Friedrich Nietzsche

....

Ⓓ Baruch Spinoza

....

FACT-CHECK This is the basic principle behind vaccines, which introduce a weakened version of infections so that the body can better fight them in the future. This approach is not recommended, however, for gunshot wounds or car accidents.

ANSWER: C. So writes Nietzsche in his fantastically subtitled book, *The Twilight of the Idols, or, How to Philosophize with a Hammer*. The line has reappeared in numerous forms since its 1889 conception.

"I don't want to belong to any club that will accept me as a member."

A Mel Brooks

B Groucho Marx

C Carol Burnett

D Gene Wilder

SEE ALSO:

"The strongest man in the world is he who stands most alone."

—HENRIK IBSEN

ANSWER: B. While it's not clear which organization it was, exactly, that Groucho resigned from with this message—perhaps it was the Friars Club—what matters is that the line became a comedy classic.

"Hope springs eternal in the human breast."

A Alexander Pope

B Harriet Beecher Stowe

C Emily Brontë

D Larry Flynt

> **WORD UP**
>
> Hope has been scientifically identified, measured, and tested in a variety of settings, from longevity to substance abuse recovery. Cicero once said, "Where there's life, there's hope." Turns out, the opposite is also true: Where there's hope, there's life.

ANSWER: A. This inspirational line comes from Pope's eighteenth-century poem *An Essay on Man*, a massive opus that aims to prove that God's creation is perfect, and that, "Whatever is, is right."

"Man is not made for defeat ... A man can be destroyed but not defeated."

A Rocky Balboa

B Mad Max

C Clint Eastwood

D Ernest Hemingway

DID YOU KNOW?

Although in popular culture it seems that defeat meant death for Roman gladiators, these bouts were not always fatal. Some combatants were spared, particularly if they gave a good show. Nice way to make a living.

ANSWER: D. Hemingway was fascinated by the perseverance of the human spirit. "The world breaks everyone and afterwards many are strong at the broken places," he wrote elsewhere.

"No one can make you feel inferior without your consent."

A David Letterman

B Shari Lewis

C Eleanor Roosevelt

D Dr. Phil

COUNTER POINT

"Thou canst not think worse of me than I do of myself."

—ROBERT BURTON

ANSWER: C. The former First Lady took an active interest in the interests of American youth—in particular their ambitions and dreams for the future. Wrote Roosevelt: "You must do the thing you think you cannot do."

"Two roads diverged in a wood, and I—I took the one less traveled by."

A Robert Frost

B Nathaniel Hawthorne

C John Denver

D William Carlos Williams

COUNTER POINT

"If you come to a fork in the road, take it." —YOGI BERRA

ANSWER: A. Though generations of students have studied this 1915 poem "The Road Not Taken" as an ode to bold nonconformity, Frost himself intended it to be ambiguous as to which road was really taken.

"Results! Why, man, I have gotten a lot of results! I know several thousand things that won't work."

A Nikola Tesla

B Thomas Edison

C Marie Curie

D Isaac Newton

SEE ALSO:

"I am always doing what I can't do yet in order to learn how to do it."

—VINCENT VAN GOGH

ANSWER: B. This inspirational statement of Edison's might be more familiar in its later, slightly snappier rendering: "I have not failed. I've just found 10,000 ways that won't work."

"Do. Or do not. There is no try."

A Sir Edmund Hillary

B Vince Lombardi

C Marcus Aurelius

D Yoda

 **COUNTER POINT** "Trying is the first step toward failure." —HOMER SIMPSON

ANSWER: D. In *The Empire Strikes Back*, Yoda challenges Luke Skywalker to use the Force to telekinetically lift his spacecraft out of a bog, motivating him with this line. Spoiler alert: Luke does.

"If there is no struggle, there is no progress."

A Jackie Robinson

B Frederick Douglass

C Malcolm X

D Steven Seagal

SEE ALSO:

"There are no gains, without pains."
—BENJAMIN FRANKLIN

ANSWER: B. Born into slavery, Douglass went on to become one of America's best-known abolitionists. For Douglass, those who desire change without agitating for it "want the ocean without the awful roar of its many waters."

"Some are born great,
some achieve greatness,
and some have greatness
thrust upon them."

Ⓐ Niccolò Machiavelli

Ⓑ Winston Churchill

Ⓒ Babe Ruth

Ⓓ William Shakespeare

COUNTER POINT

"Some men are born mediocre,
some men achieve mediocrity,
and some men have mediocrity
thrust upon them."

—JOSEPH HELLER

ANSWER: D. So says Malvolio in Shakespeare's comedy *Twelfth Night.*
Although the line is often quoted in inspirational contexts, Malvolio is
actually a bit of a fool who serves as the object of pranks and ridicule.

"If you feel alone and by yourself, look in the mirror and wow— there's two of you!"

A Stuart Smalley

B Tony Robbins

C Shaquille O'Neal

D Pee-wee Herman

SEE ALSO:

"You're your best thing."

—TONI MORRISON

ANSWER: C. Basketball great, film actor, and television personality O'Neal can add another profession to his career: self-help guru. He imparted this sage piece of advice on his official Twitter page.

"Nothing contributes so much to tranquilize the mind as a steady purpose—a point on which the soul may fix its intellectual eye."

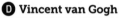

A Mary Shelley

B Edgar Allan Poe

C Augusto Pinochet

D Vincent van Gogh

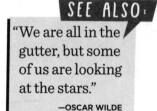

SEE ALSO:

"We are all in the gutter, but some of us are looking at the stars."

—OSCAR WILDE

ANSWER: A. This line appears at the start of Shelley's novel *Frankenstein,* in which an explorer named Robert Walton describes meeting one Victor Frankenstein during an Arctic expedition.

"Give me but one firm spot on which to stand, and I will move the earth."

A Hercules

B Archimedes

C James Watt, inventor of the steam engine

D Euclid

DID YOU KNOW?

According to lore, if everyone on one side of the planet jumped at the same time, the planet would wobble out of orbit. Turns out, well—no. Even if every living human hopped in exactly the same spot, Earth would move only an infinitesimal amount.

ANSWER: B. In addition to his pioneering work in mathematics, Archimedes was also a prolific inventor and physicist. According to later accounts, this statement was how the ancient Greek illustrated the power of the lever.

"If you will it, it is no dream."

A Romulus

B Susan B. Anthony

C Theodor Herzl

D Aung San Suu Kyi

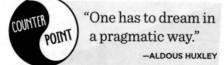

COUNTER POINT

"One has to dream in a pragmatic way."

—ALDOUS HUXLEY

ANSWER: C. Herzl's 1897 founding of the World Zionist Organization laid the groundwork for the formation of the state of Israel—though he did not live to see it through. This axiom became a Zionist slogan.

"It is the same with people as it is with riding a bike. Only when moving can one comfortably maintain one's balance."

A Madeleine Albright

B Lance Armstrong

C Elizabeth Taylor

D Albert Einstein

DID YOU KNOW?

In 2017, American cyclist Amanda Coker set a world record by cycling 100,000 miles in just 423 days. That's an average of 236 miles per day.

ANSWER: D. The great physicist included this proviso in a 1930 letter to his son, Eduard. Sadly, he had a difficult time maintaining balance—a schizophrenic, Eduard spent the majority of his life in the care of others.

"If I have seen further it is by standing on the shoulders of giants."

Ⓐ Mary Lou Retton

Ⓑ Ludwig van Beethoven

Ⓒ Isaac Newton

Ⓓ John Coltrane

DID YOU KNOW?

If you stood on the shoulders of the tallest recorded man ever to live, your feet would be nearly nine feet off the ground. Robert Pershing Wadlow, born 1918, stood 8 feet, 11 inches at his tallest.

ANSWER: C. Widely credited for founding modern physics—and for theorizing the force of gravity—Newton also produced volumes of work on theology, mathematics, and optics. He must have stood on quite a few shoulders.

"Ever tried. Ever failed. No matter. Try again. Fail again. Fail better."

A Samuel Beckett

B George Washington Carver

C Alexander Graham Bell

D e. e. cummings

DID YOU KNOW?

Several awards exist for failures. The Razzies celebrate the worst of Hollywood. The Darwin Awards, meanwhile, honor those who "significantly improve the gene pool by eliminating themselves from the human race in an obviously stupid way."

ANSWER: A. This line appears in the novelist and playwright's late prose piece, "Worstward Ho." "Fail better" has since become an inspirational maxim in Silicon Valley, where far more startups fail than succeed.

–ISMS

E veryone might get their fifteen minutes of fame, but few people get so many as fifteen famous quotes to their name. In fact, most big names only have a couple chestnuts worth remembering. Yet the likes of Dolly Parton and Yogi Berra didn't leave behind just a few choice quotes, but a whole genre of sayings all their own. This select group of quotable notables warrant their own suffix, and their own category: –isms.

Each of the following quizzes presents eight quotes. Four will be genuine –isms. The other four will either be misattributed to them or completely made up. It's your job to separate the phonies from the real McCoys.

BUSH-*isms*

America's 43rd president, **George W. Bush**, said only half of the following quotations. Which of them are the real Bush-isms?

1. "Families is where our nation finds hope, where wings take dream."

2. "The internet that Americans get is just like the Mexican internet, only it isn't in Mexican."

3. "Fool me once, shame on—shame on you. Fool me—you can't get fooled again."

4. "Too many OB/GYNs aren't able to practice their love with women all across the country."

5. "For every child wishing for a brighter future, I have one word for you: energy independence."

6. "I met with the Australian prime minister to feel him up on the matter—and, uh, the feeling is good."

7. "I know how hard it is for you to put food on your family."

8. "When the going gets tough, the tough have to get even tougher, so we're going to get tough."

Answer: 1-True, 2-False, 3-True, 4-True, 5-False, 6-False, 7-True, 8-False

DOLLY-*isms*

Country star **Dolly Parton** said only half of the following quotations. Which of them are the real Dolly-isms?

1. "**Ninety-nine percent of the world's lovers are not with their first choice. That's what makes the jukebox play.**"

2. "**I got used to men staring. Sure, my eyes are up here, but my heart isn't.**"

3. "**God and I have a great relationship, but we both see other people.**"

4. "**A good country song tells a story. A great country song tells a *different* story.**"

5. "I know some of the best Dolly Parton jokes. I made 'em up myself."

6. "Burt [Reynolds] and I never saw eye to eye—unless there was a phone book I could stand on."

7. "The dumb blonde act didn't bother me because I know I'm not dumb—and I know I'm not blonde, either."

8. "If I see something sagging, dragging, or bagging, I'm going to have the stuff tucked or plucked."

Answer: 1-False, 2-False, 3-True, 4-False, 5-True, 6-False, 7-True, 8-True

ALI-*isms*

Renowned boxer and social activist **Muhammad Ali** said only half of the following quotations. Which of them are the real Ali-isms?

1. "Viet Cong, King Kong, it all sounds like monkey business to me."

2. "Grass grows, birds fly, waves pound the sand. I beat people up."

3. "Float like a butterfly, sting like a bee."

4. "I don't intend to hurt Joe Frazier. He'll be out before he feels a thing."

5. "The man who views the world at fifty the same as he did at twenty has wasted thirty years of his life."

6. "Everybody has a plan until they get punched in the mouth."

7. "I should be a postage stamp. That's the only way I'll ever get licked."

8. "Impossible is just a big word thrown around by small men."

MARX-*isms*

Groucho Marx, the mustachioed funnyman and leader of the Marx Brothers comedy troupe, said only half of the following quotations. Which of them are the real Marx-isms?

1. "Darling, with you I couldn't be happier. Though I could be happier without you."

2. "From the moment I picked up your book until I laid it down, I was convulsed with laughter. Someday I intend reading it."

3. "Quick, someone find a doctor. This man has just survived a heart attack and we need something that'll really do him in."

4. "Your average moviegoer isn't just some poor sucker. Most of them are decently well-off suckers."

5. "I must say I find television very educational. The minute somebody turns it on, I go into the library and read a good book."

6. "I never forget a face, but in your case I'll be glad to make an exception."

7. "Time flies like an arrow. Fruit flies like a banana."

8. "To write an autobiography of Groucho Marx would be as asinine as to read an autobiography of Groucho Marx."

Answer: 1-False, 2-True, 3-False, 4-False, 5-True, 6-True, 7-False, 8-True

PARKER-*isms*

Dorothy Parker, the much-imitated writer and shining wit of the Roaring Twenties, said only half of the following quotations. Which of them are the real Parker-isms?

1. "Brevity is the soul of lingerie."

2. "If you can't say something good about someone, sit right here by me."

3. "Take me or leave me; or, as is the usual order of things, both."

4. "Idle hands may be the devil's workshop, but it's busy ones get you in trouble."

5. "I'm as pure as the driven slush."

6. [Telegram declining party invitation] "Tell them I got tired. Laid myself out. Or vice versa."

7. "Scratch a lover, and find a foe."

8. [Epitaph for herself] "Excuse my dust."

YOGI-*isms*

Yogi Berra, baseball Hall of Famer and master of the mangled malapropism, said only half of the following quotations. Which of them are the real Yogi-isms?

1. "It ain't over 'til it's over."

2. "It ain't over 'til the fat lady sings."

3. [Upon being asked, "What's the point of baseball?"] "Most of 'em I've seen are round."

4. "You can observe a lot by watchin'."

5. "I try keeping my mouth shut, but no one listens."

6. [Upon being asked for the time] "You mean now?"

7. "I really didn't say everything I said."

8. "If you really want my opinion, I'll take yours."

7-True, 8-False

Answer: 1-True, 2-False, 3-False, 4-True, 5-False, 6-True,

KING-*isms*

Widely celebrated for his civil rights activism, **Martin Luther King Jr.** is also a magnet for misattributions and said only half of the following quotations. Which of them are the real King-isms?

1. "I regard myself as a soldier, though a soldier of peace."

2. "You can't separate peace from freedom because no one can be at peace unless he has his freedom."

3. "Injustice anywhere is a threat to justice everywhere."

4. [After a bad flight] "I don't want to give you the impression that as a Baptist preacher I don't have faith in God in the air—it's simply that I've had more experience with Him on the ground."

5. "I will not rejoice in the death of one, not even an enemy."

6. "I want to be the white man's brother, not his brother-in-law."

7. "I also have a dream that my four little children will learn to wipe their feet before entering the house, but that's another matter."

8. "If a man hasn't discovered something he will die for, he isn't fit to live."

Answer: 1-False, 2-False, 3-True, 4-True, 5-False, 6-True, 7-False, 8-True

THATCHER-*isms*

Margaret Thatcher, the first female prime minister of the United Kingdom and an ideological kindred spirit of Ronald Reagan's, said only half of the following quotations. Which of them are the real Thatcher-isms?

1. "Being powerful is like being a lady. If you have to tell people you are, you aren't."

2. "There is no such thing as society."

3. "No woman in my time will be Prime Minister."

4. "In a democracy, it's up to our free markets to decide how much milk a child ought to get."

5. "We have heard for too long the chattering of the naysayers. Today, it ends; we have made our figgy pudding—where is yours?"

6. "You may call me Prime Minister, and you may call me Iron Lady, but 'Mags' seems a bit familiar, doesn't it, Mr. Reagan?"

7. "To those waiting with bated breath for that favorite media catchphrase, the U-turn, I have only this to say. 'You turn if you want to; the lady's not for turning.'"

8. "In politics, if you want anything said, ask a man; if you want anything done, ask a woman."

Answer: 1-False, 2-True, 3-True, 4-False, 5-False, 6-False, 7-True, 8-True

TWAIN-*isms*

The grandfather of American letters, **Mark Twain**, said a lot of things. He also didn't say a lot of things people say he said, including half of the following quotations. Which of them are the real Twain-isms?

1. "Training is everything. The peach was once a bitter almond; cauliflower is nothing but cabbage with a college education."

2. "It's not the size of the dog in the fight; it's the size of the fight in the dog."

3. "Adam and Eve might have found a good lawyer if they knew where to look. After all, it was on the fifth day God made the creeping things."

4. "It is better to keep your mouth shut and appear stupid than to open it and remove all doubt."

5. "Everything human is pathetic. The secret source of humor itself is not joy but sorrow. There is no humor in heaven."

6. "Always do right. This will gratify some people and astonish the rest."

7. "When angry, count four; when very angry, swear."

8. "Some readers suffer the delusion that I based Tom Sawyer on myself. In truth it's the other way around."

Answer: 1-True, 2-False, 3-False, 4-False, 5-True, 6-True, 7-True, 8-False

MARTHA-*isms*

Martha Stewart basically invented the concept of a lifestyle brand, and in the process taught millions of Americans how to live better—but said only half of the following quotations. Which of them are the real Martha-isms?

1. "The secret of entertaining is simply to be yourself. That is, until the guests arrive."

2. "We're all trying to do the same thing: live well."

3. "You could spend a week on a pilgrimage or meditation retreat—or you could make organic goat's milk soap bars."

4. "Of course I know how to roll a joint."

5. "I didn't enjoy being incarcerated, but it did teach me certain crafts—you wouldn't believe what I can do with a toothbrush handle."

6. "I catnap now and then . . . but I think while I nap, so it's not a waste of time."

7. "Always take a bath before and after [sex] . . . and don't forget to brush your teeth."

8. "To do exactly as your neighbors do is the only sensible rule."

Answer: 1-False, 2-True, 3-False, 4-True, 5-False, 6-True, 7-True, 8-False

AGING

"I think I'll be happy to die before I get old, or after I get old, or any time in between. I sound like a f***ing greetings card."

—PETE TOWNSHEND

"Live long and prosper."

A Moses

B Yoda

C Spock

D Mao Zedong

DID YOU KNOW?

The country with the highest proportion of centenarians in the world is Japan. In 1963, 153 Japanese people had reached age 100; today, that number is over 65,000.

ANSWER: C. *Star Trek*'s Vulcan salute includes both this saying and a hand gesture with a part between the middle and ring fingers. Leonard Nimoy, who played Spock, derived the gesture from a traditional Jewish blessing.

"It's sad to grow old— but nice to ripen."

A Anjelica Huston

B Brigitte Bardot

C Carmen Miranda

D Dean Martin

SEE ALSO:

> "We turn not older
> with years, but
> newer every day."
> —EMILY DICKINSON

ANSWER: B. The French blonde bombshell turned toward animal rights after retiring from the entertainment world in 1973.

"Don't look back. Something might be gaining on you."

A John Madden

B Rodney Dangerfield

C Lucille Ball

D Satchel Paige

SEE ALSO:

"Old age isn't so bad when you consider the alternative."

—MAURICE CHEVALIER
(popularized by)

ANSWER: D. After an unmatched career in the Negro Leagues, the sharp-witted pitcher made his Major League Baseball debut at 42. His advice for staying young: "Avoid running at all times."

AGING
258

"Every man over forty is a scoundrel."

A Vladimir Nabokov

B George Bernard Shaw

C Hugh Hefner

D Monica Lewinsky

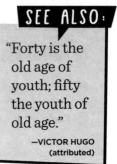

SEE ALSO:

"Forty is the old age of youth; fifty the youth of old age."

—VICTOR HUGO (attributed)

ANSWER: B. Shaw's *Maxims for Revolutionists* contains this striking line, as well as: "Youth, which is forgiven everything, forgives itself nothing; age, which forgives itself everything, is forgiven nothing."

"Nature gives you the face you have at twenty; life shapes the face you have at thirty; but at fifty, you get the face you deserve."

A Coco Chanel

B Auguste Rodin

C Annie Leibovitz

D Rudyard Kipling

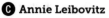

"Looking fifty is great— if you're sixty." —JOAN RIVERS

ANSWER: A. The haute couture pioneer—only recently revealed to have been a Nazi agent during World War II—maintained that old women as well as young should avail themselves of the latest fashions.

"The past is never dead. It's not even past."

A William Faulkner

B Babe Ruth

C Barack Obama

D Scarlett O'Hara

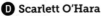
DID YOU KNOW?

This is particularly so for believers in reincarnation. Egyptologist Dorothy Eady, for instance, claimed to use her past life as the mistress to an ancient Egyptian king to guide her work. Though her colleagues doubted the story, they did commend her scholarship.

ANSWER: A. One of Faulkner's best-known lines, it appears in his 1951 novel *Requiem for a Nun*, set in the writer's fictional Yoknapatawpha County, Mississippi.

"I grow old . . . I grow old . . . I shall wear the bottoms of my trousers rolled."

Ⓐ W. B. Yeats

Ⓑ T. S. Eliot

Ⓒ Ebenezer Scrooge

Ⓓ William Blake

> **SEE ALSO:**
>
> "Old age. It's the only disease . . . that you don't look forward to being cured of."
>
> —FROM *CITIZEN KANE*

ANSWER: B. These lines come near the end of Eliot's first professionally published poem, "The Love Song of J. Alfred Prufrock," a portrait of a middle-aged man coming to terms with his own mediocrity.

"Ain't nothing an old man can do for me but bring me a message from a young one."

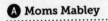

A Moms Mabley

B Zora Neale Hurston

C Dolly Parton

D Sojourner Truth

DID YOU KNOW?

The world record for the oldest confirmed couple ever to wed is held by Brits George and Doreen Kirby, whose combined age on the day of their nuptials was 194 years.

ANSWER: A. Born Loretta Mary Aiken, Mabley left home in her teens to join the Chitlin' Circuit of African American vaudeville and continued working into her seventies—at which time she found renewed fame on 1960s television.

"Those who cannot remember the past are condemned to repeat it."

A Elie Wiesel

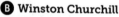

B Winston Churchill

C Edmund Burke

D George Santayana

COUNTER POINT

"That men do not learn very much from the lessons of history is the most important of all the lessons that history has to teach." —ALDOUS HUXLEY

ANSWER: D. This widely quoted—and widely misattributed—quotation comes from the Spanish philosopher's 1905 work *The Life of Reason.*

"Old age is the most unexpected of all the things that can happen to a man."

A Jimmy Carter

B Leon Trotsky

C Morgan Freeman

D Obi-Wan Kenobi
(*Star Wars*)

SEE ALSO:

"A person is always startled when he hears himself seriously called an old man for the first time."

—OLIVER WENDELL HOLMES SR.

ANSWER: B. The Russian revolutionary jotted this thought down in his diaries while exiled in Mexico. The process of aging, however, probably came as less of a surprise than his grisly assassination a few years after writing this.

"A man has every season while a woman only has the right to spring."

A Jane Fonda

B Nina Simone

C Simone de Beauvoir

D Abigail Adams

COUNTER POINT

"No spring nor summer beauty hath such grace as I have seen in one autumnal face."
—JOHN DONNE

ANSWER: A. Broadway player, Hollywood star, antiwar activist, fitness guru, and memoirist, Fonda has managed to prove the exception to her own rule.

"An old man is twice a child."

Ⓐ William Shakespeare

Ⓑ Samuel Johnson

Ⓒ Ivan Pavlov

Ⓓ Benjamin Button

Researchers have found that sufferers of dementia lose their faculties in the same order that children acquire them.

ANSWER: A. Shakespeare enjoyed this conceit—elsewhere he called old age "second childishness." Yet the idea wasn't new. "When a man reaches the last stage of life," wrote Roman playwright Plautus around 200 BCE, "they say that he has grown a child again."

"Do not go gentle into that good night."

A Ernest Shackleton

B T. S. Eliot

C Dylan Thomas

D Alice Walker

DID YOU KNOW?

Scientists have found that those who maintain a specific goal or purpose in their life reliably tend to live longer and stay healthier.

ANSWER: C. Dylan Thomas's most famous poem "Do not go gentle into that good night" is furious affirmation of the will to live. Sadly, the Welshman himself succumbed early: A prolific drinker, he died at just 39.

"I used to think getting old was about vanity, but actually it's about losing people you love. Getting wrinkles is trivial."

A Nancy Reagan

B Ella Fitzgerald

C Ian McKellen

D Joyce Carol Oates

SEE ALSO:

"Old age is . . . a lot of crossed-off names in an address book."

—RONALD BLYTHE

ANSWER: D. The author of more than fifty novels—ten of which were published in her seventies—Oates has lost none of her fecundity in later years.

DIFFICULTY LEVEL

"Once you're over the hill, you begin to pick up speed."

A Bob Hope

B Muhammad Ali

C Charles M. Schulz

D Joan Rivers

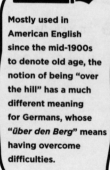

WORD UP

Mostly used in American English since the mid-1900s to denote old age, the notion of being "over the hill" has a much different meaning for Germans, whose *"über den Berg"* means having overcome difficulties.

ANSWER: C. The cartoonist continued drawing *Peanuts* well into his seventies. As Schulz said upon retiring: "I am now older than people I used to think were old. It's a little disconcerting."

AGING

270

"As you get older, the pickings get slimmer, but the people sure don't."

A Eddie Murphy

B Julia Child

C Carrie Fisher

D Whoopi Goldberg

FACT-CHECK Even among athletes, age-related weight gain is something of an inevitability. One study found that every decade adds a little over three pounds to the average 6-foot man—and that's just for avid runners.

ANSWER: C. Fisher rose to super-stardom in just her second studio film, the sci-fi mega-hit *Star Wars*, in which she played Princess Leia. She would go on to reprise the role nearly forty years later.

"I'll never make the mistake of being seventy again."

A Casey Stengel

B Mahatma Gandhi

C John Cleese

D Queen Elizabeth the Queen Mother

COUNTER POINT

"Oh, to be seventy again!"

—ATTRIBUTED TO FRENCH STATESMAN GEORGES CLEMENCEAU, upon seeing an attractive woman on his eightieth birthday

ANSWER: A. The legendary wit said this upon being relieved of his job as Yankees manager due to age. A favorite line of his now adorns his grave marker: "There comes a time in every man's life and I've had plenty of them."

> "This *long run* is a misleading guide to current affairs. *In the long run* we are all dead."

A Barry Goldwater

B Tyler Durden (*Fight Club*)

C John Maynard Keynes

D Arthur Schopenhauer

FACT-CHECK

Though this maxim hasn't been disproven yet, Silicon Valley entrepreneurs think mortality is ripe for disruption. Numerous startups have emerged in the past decade aiming to beat aging.

ANSWER: C. Perhaps the most influential economist of the twentieth century, Keynes founded modern macroeconomics and was also a popular essayist.

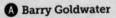

DIFFICULTY LEVEL

"In the unconscious, every one of us is convinced of his own immortality."

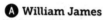 **A** William James

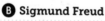 **B** Sigmund Freud

C Luis Buñuel

D Leonardo da Vinci

SEE ALSO:

"Nobody is so old that he does not think he could live another year."

—CICERO

ANSWER: B. The father of psychoanalysis held that deep in our minds was a reservoir of memories and feelings called the unconscious. "At bottom," Freud wrote, "no one believes in his own death."

"In a dream you are never eighty."

A Anne Sexton

....

B Gabriel García Márquez

....

C Lauren Bacall

....

D Jacques Lacan

....

SEE ALSO:

"Life would be infinitely happier if we could only be born at the age of eighty and gradually approach eighteen."

—MARK TWAIN

ANSWER: A. Part of the Confessional school of American poets, Sexton began writing in 1957 at the suggestion of her therapist. Three years later she had published her debut collection, *To Bedlam and Part Way Back*.

"It's better to burn out than to fade away."

A Neil Young

....

B Kurt Cobain

....

C James Dean

....

D Amy Winehouse

SEE ALSO:

"I would rather that my spark should burn out in a brilliant blaze than it should be stifled by dry-rot."

—JACK LONDON

ANSWER: A. The Canadian rocker included this lyric in his song "Hey Hey, My My (Into the Black)," from the 1979 album *Rust Never Sleeps*. The line would later achieve infamy when it appeared in Kurt Cobain's suicide note.

"I have four reasons for not writing: I am too old, too fat, too lazy, and too rich."

A Orson Welles

B David Hume

C Marlon Brando

D William Howard Taft

It's never too late to begin writing. The oldest literary late bloomer on record was Bertha Wood, who in 2005 published a memoir telling the story of her life as a holiday camp operator in England. She was 100.

ANSWER: B. One of the most widely read writers of his age, the Scottish historian and philosopher faced requests in his later years to add another volume to his popular History of England series. This was how he declined.

"The tragedy of old age is not that one is old, but that one is young."

A Gustave Flaubert

B Gandalf (*The Lord of the Rings*)

C Oscar Wilde

D Toni Morrison

COUNTER POINT

"The great thing about getting older is that you don't lose all the other ages you've been."

—MADELEINE L'ENGLE

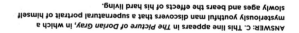

ANSWER: C. This line appears in *The Picture of Dorian Gray*, in which a mysteriously youthful man discovers that a supernatural portrait of himself slowly ages and bears the effects of his hard living.

"I only ever had one wrinkle and I'm sitting on it."

A Don Rickles

B Katharine Hepburn

C Jeanne Calment, oldest person on record

D Ruth Bader Ginsburg

SEE ALSO:

"There are no wrinkles in the heart."

—JULIETTE DROUET

ANSWER: C. This is one of the numerous *bon mots* attributed to the record-setting Calment, who died in 1997 at 122 years old. The Frenchwoman chalked her longevity up to olive oil and red wine.

"Wrinkles should merely indicate where smiles have been."

Ⓐ Jacqueline Kennedy Onassis

Ⓑ Phyllis Diller

Ⓒ Mark Twain

Ⓓ Rembrandt

SEE ALSO:

"Age imprints more wrinkles in the mind than it does on the face."

—MICHEL DE MONTAIGNE

ANSWER: C. Twain kept his sharp wit into old age, publishing his final novel in his early seventies. As he wrote in his autobiography: "I was young and foolish then; now I am old and foolisher."

"It's nice to be here. When you're ninety-nine years old, it's nice to be anywhere."

A Irving Berlin

B George Burns

C Kirk Douglas

D Bob Hope

SEE ALSO:

"To an old man any place that's warm is homeland."

—MAXIM GORKY

ANSWER: B. Burns began his entertainment career at the age of seven. He went on to find stardom in vaudeville, radio, film, and eventually television, defining generations of American comedy. He lived to 100.

AGING

281

"It's not the years, honey. It's the mileage."

 A Indiana Jones (*Raiders of the Lost Ark*)

B Helen Gurley Brown

 C Dale Earnhardt

 D Angela Lansbury

SEE ALSO:

"Age is a question of mind over matter. If you don't mind, it doesn't matter."

—SATCHEL PAIGE (attributed)

ANSWER: A. This is how Harrison Ford, star of the Indiana Jones films, famously responds to love interest Marion Ravenwood (Karen Allen) after she remarks at how much he had changed since their last meeting.

"I recently turned sixty. Practically a third of my life is over."

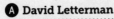

Ⓐ David Letterman

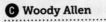

Ⓑ Keith Richards

Ⓒ Woody Allen

Ⓓ Betty White

FACT-CHECK No one on record has made it as far as the 180 years implied in this quote, but in the biblical tradition, life spans in the centuries are commonplace. The granddaddy of them all: Methuselah, who lived 969 years.

ANSWER: C. Allen's films have continued to resonate thanks to his incomparable wit and unique take on the human condition.

AGING

283

DIFFICULTY LEVEL

"Beauty fades, dumb is forever."

A R. Lee Ermey

B Piers Morgan

C Charles Barkley

D Judith "Judge Judy" Sheindlin

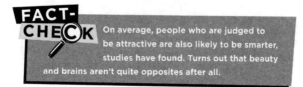

FACT-CHECK

On average, people who are judged to be attractive are also likely to be smarter, studies have found. Turns out that beauty and brains aren't quite opposites after all.

ANSWER: D. Judge Judy made her first television appearance at age 52. The reality show host's sharp tongue has made her one of the highest-paid personalities on television, earning a reported annual salary of $47 million.

"Getting old ain't for sissies."

A Johnny Cash

B Mr. T

C Bette Davis

D Harry S. Truman

DID YOU KNOW?

Despite the many slings and arrows that come with aging, there is a silver lining: The elderly tend to have lower rates of anxiety and sadness than the general population. Golden years, indeed.

ANSWER: C. Actor Paul Newman attributed this line to Davis, who left behind a film career spanning more than five decades. "I would never stop," she told an interviewer at age 80. "Relax? I relax when I work. It's my life."

PHILIP
ROTH

Madonna

$0

$0

HEAD-TO-HEAD

Everyone wants to be unique. But even when artists and celebrities attempt to forge a new style, they inevitably end up echoing others who have come before them. Whether it's because of direct imitation, unconscious influence, or the fact that all massive egoists sound pretty much the same, it can be kinda hard to differentiate between the words of, say, Kanye West and Salvador Dalí, or Kurt Vonnegut and Taylor Swift. Thus Head-to-Head.

In this mini-game, you'll be presented with eight quotes. It's your job to decide which four come from Person A and which four from Person B. After all, there's nothing new under the sun.

BENITO MUSSOLINI

VS

WERNER HERZOG

Benito Mussolini, a chief architect of European fascism, ruled Italy through World War II. **Werner Herzog** is an audacious German filmmaker whose work explores the furthest extremes of human ability and the natural world. Which of them said the following?

· · · · ·

1. "I want to make my existence a masterpiece."

2. "You can fight a rumor only with an even wilder rumor."

3. "A man in my position must be stupid at least once a week, or must seem so. On such days I learn a great deal."

4. "You hate me because you still love me."

5. "The common denominator of the universe is not harmony, but chaos, hostility, and murder."

6. "There are dignified stupidities, and there are heroic stupidities, and there is such a thing as stupid stupidities."

7. "We have to articulate ourselves. Otherwise we would be cows in the field."

8. "War is to man what motherhood is to a woman. From a philosophical and doctrinal viewpoint, I do not believe in perpetual peace."

JERRY SEINFELD

VS

TINA FEY

J erry Seinfeld, the standup performer and
star of the hit sitcom *Seinfeld*, is one of the
defining comedians of the 1990s. **Tina Fey**,
creator of the show *30 Rock* and author of the
bestselling *Bossypants*, is one of the defining
comedians of the 2000s. Which of them said the
following?

· · · · ·

1. "You can tell how smart people are by what
   they laugh at."

2. "Confidence is a fascinating commodity.
   There's no upper limit on the usefulness of
   it, as long as it doesn't bleed into arrogance."

3. "Where lipstick is concerned, the important thing is not color, but to accept God's final word on where your lips end."

4. "Do your thing and don't care if they like it."

5. "If you want to make an audience laugh, you dress a man up like an old lady and push her down the stairs. If you want to make comedy writers laugh, you push an actual old lady down the stairs."

6. "The definition of crazy in show business is a woman who keeps talking even after no one wants to f*** her anymore."

7. "Sometimes the road less traveled is less traveled for a reason."

8. "In my world, the wronger something feels, the righter it is."

KURT VONNEGUT

VS

TAYLOR SWIFT

Kurt Vonnegut was a distinguished science-fiction author known for his gentle, world-weary humor. **Taylor Swift** is a country-singer-turned-mega-pop-star with a ravenous audience of teenage fans. Which of them said the following?

• • • • •

1. "We are what we pretend to be, so we must be careful about what we pretend to be."

2. "No matter what happens in life, be good to people."

3. "All we are is skin and bone, trained to get along."

4. "Everything was beautiful and nothing hurt."

5. "Life is a tough crowd."

6. "Words can break people into a million pieces, but they can also put them back together."

7. "I want to stand as close to the edge as I can without going over."

8. "There is love enough in this world for everybody, if people will just look."

Answer: 1-KV, 2-TS, 3-TS, 4-KV, 5-TS, 6-TS, 7-KV, 8-KV

DONALD TRUMP

VS

SILVIO BERLUSCONI

Donald Trump is an American business tycoon-turned-politician with an outsize ego and a weakness for beautiful women. **Silvio Berlusconi** is an Italian business tycoon-turned-politician with an outsize ego and a weakness for beautiful women. Which of them said the following?

. . . . .

1. "Part of the beauty of me is that I am very rich."

2. "Do it my way and earn more money."

3. "More important than the mouth is the brain."

4. "I have little hair because my brain is so big it pushes the hair out."

5. "I am the most legally persecuted man of all times, in the whole history of mankind, worldwide."

6. "My fingers are long and beautiful, as, it has been well documented, are various other parts of my body."

7. "I am the Jesus Christ of politics . . . I sacrifice myself for everyone."

8. "The concept of shaking hands is absolutely terrible, and statistically I've been proven right."

LADY GAGA
VS
SLAVOJ ZIZEK

Lady Gaga is a pop star whose Top-40 hits and ever-shifting creative identities have earned her legions of fans known as "Little Monsters." **Slavoj Žižek** is a Slovenian philosopher nicknamed "the Elvis of cultural theory" for his entertaining style and use of popular culture. Which of them said the following?

· · · · ·

1. "What makes us happy is not to get what we want, but to dream about it."

2. "I'm telling you a lie in a vicious effort that you will repeat my lie over and over until it becomes true."

3. "There is something real in the illusion, more real than in the reality behind it."

4. "I am not human. I am a monster."

5. "I'm not real. I'm theater. And you and I—this is just rehearsal."

6. "I embrace pop culture. The very thing that everybody says is poisonous and ostentatious and shallow, it's like my chemistry book."

7. "As artists, we are eternally heartbroken."

8. "I am not myself. I do all my work to escape myself."

OSAMA BIN LADEN
VS
MAGNETO

Osama bin Laden orchestrated the terror attacks of September 11, 2001, which killed nearly 3,000 Americans. **Magneto**, a character in the X-Men superhero franchise, is a superpowered mutant who spearheads an insurgency to overthrow humanity. Which of them said the following?

. . . . .

1. "Whatever comes, I and mine will not go like lambs to the slaughter—but like tigers."

2. "I have sworn to only live free. Even if I find bitter the taste of death, I don't want to die humiliated or deceived."

3. "Make no mistake, my brothers. They will draw first blood. . . . The only question is, will you join my brotherhood and fight, or wait for the inevitable genocide?"

4. "Free men do not forfeit their security."

5. "In today's wars, there are no morals."

6. "Just as you lay waste to our nation, so shall we lay waste to yours."

7. "They have their weapons, we have ours. We will strike with a vengeance and a fury that this world has never witnessed."

8. "There is no land of tolerance. There is no peace."

Answer: 1-M, 2-ObL, 3-M, 4-ObL, 5-ObL, 6-ObL, 7-M, 8-M

KANYE WEST

VS

SALVADOR DALÍ

Kanye West is a rapper and producer whose volatile public persona and multi-platinum albums have made him a modern-day icon. **Salvador Dalí** was a twentieth-century painter and lifelong eccentric who popularized surrealism. Which of them said the following?

• • • • •

1. "I don't have fangs. I'm a porcupine. I'm a blowfish."

2. "When I talk it's like a painting."

3. "I don't do drugs. I am drugs."

4. "When you're a genius, you don't have the right to die, because we are necessary for the progress of humanity."

5. "I'm a postmodernist, at best, as a career. I'm a futurist mentally."

6. "The sole difference between myself and a madman is the fact that I am not mad."

7. "It is not necessary for the public to know whether I am joking or whether I am serious."

8. "I think people think I like to think a lot. And I don't. I do not like to think at all."

HOMER SIMPSON

VS

W. C. FIELDS

Homer Simpson is the inept, boorish, and lovable patriarch in the animated sitcom *The Simpsons*. **W. C. Fields** was a comedian with a stage persona as a hard-drinking, child-hating curmudgeon known for the tagline: "Never give a sucker an even break." Which of them said the following?

· · · · ·

1. "Don't say you can't swear off drinking. It's easy—I've done it a thousand times."

2. "A woman is like a beer. They smell good, they look good, you'd step over your own mother just to get one."

3. [On children] "When I see the smiles on their little faces, I just know they're getting ready to jab me with something."

4. "You kids are disgusting, skulking around here all day, reeking of popcorn and lollipops."

5. "Weaseling out of things is important to learn. It's what separates us from the animals—except the weasel."

6. "Just because I don't care doesn't mean I'm not listening."

7. "A thing worth having is worth cheating for."

8. "Women are like elephants to me; I like to look at them, but I wouldn't want to own one."

BENJAMIN FRANKLIN

VS

FRIEDRICH NIETZSCHE

Benjamin Franklin was an American statesman who wrote the popular *Poor Richard's Almanack* before helping found the United States. **Friedrich Nietzsche** was a German philosopher who grappled with nihilism and famously declared, "God is dead!" Which of them said the following?

· · · · ·

1. "He does not possess wealth; it possesses him."

2. "What good is a newborn baby?"

3. "A good marriage is founded on the talent for friendship."

4. "Man does not strive for happiness; only the Englishman does that."

5. "He that falls in love with himself will have no rivals."

6. "Keep your eyes wide open before marriage, half shut afterwards."

7. "One must have a good memory to be able to keep the promises one makes."

8. "Convictions are more dangerous enemies of truth than lies."

MADONNA

VS

PHILIP ROTH

Madonna is a multitalented actress and recording artist whose breakout 1980s hits combined Catholic imagery and sexual provocation. **Philip Roth** was a Pulitzer Prize–winning novelist whose writing explored the Jewish identity and repressed male desire. Which of them said the following?

. . . . .

1. "Rejection is the greatest aphrodisiac."

2. "I always thought of losing my virginity as a career move."

3. "To become a celebrity is to become a brand name."

4. "When in doubt, act like God."

5. "Maybe the best thing would be to forget being right or wrong about people and just go along for the ride. But if you can do that—well, lucky you."

6. "I'm exactly the opposite of religious, I'm anti-religious. I find religious people hideous."

7. "I wouldn't have turned out the way I was if I didn't have all those old-fashioned values to rebel against."

8. "They boo you, they whistle, they stamp their feet—you hate it but you thrive on it. Because the things that wear you down are the things that nurture you and your talent."

Answer: 1-M, 2-M, 3-PR, 4-M, 5-PR, 6-PR, 7-M, 8-PR

WISDOM & MISCELLANY

"Men are sometimes hanged for telling the truth."

—JOAN OF ARC

"The unexamined life is not worth living."

A Ralph Waldo Emerson

B Aesop

C Socrates

D Ivan Turgenev

FACT-CHECK

People actually do a pretty poor job at self-examination. One massive study, aimed at comparing how people judge themselves versus how they really perform, found that, at best, "people have only moderate insight into their abilities." And yet we persist.

ANSWER: C. Plato's account of his mentor's final days includes this immortal dictum, part of Socrates's attempt to convince authorities that his itinerant philosophizing was not corrupting the youth of Athens.

"I yam what I yam and that's all that I yam."

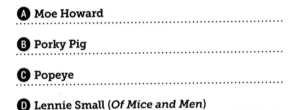

A Moe Howard

B Porky Pig

C Popeye

D Lennie Small (*Of Mice and Men*)

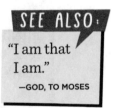

SEE ALSO:

"I am that I am."

—GOD, TO MOSES

ANSWER: C. Introduced by original *Popeye* cartoonist E. C. Segar in 1931, this line eventually became the motto of the big-armed, spinach-eating sailor man.

"The surest sign that intelligent life exists elsewhere in the universe is that none of it has tried to contact us."

 A Bill Watterson (*Calvin and Hobbes*)

B Carl Sagan

C Jon Stewart

D Buzz Aldrin

 **SEE ALSO:**

"It is not clear that intelligence has any long-term survival value."

—STEPHEN HAWKING

ANSWER: A. The six-year-old comic character and his feline companion—named for philosophers John Calvin and Thomas Hobbes—regularly pondered the depths of the human condition.

"When you stare for a long time into an abyss, the abyss stares back into you."

Ⓐ Hannah Arendt

Ⓑ Friedrich Nietzsche

Ⓒ Jacques Cousteau

Ⓓ Søren Kierkegaard

> **WORD UP** 🖊
>
> *Abyss* derives originally from the Greek *a* (without) + *byssos* (bottom). An abyss, then, is literally bottomless, though the word can refer to anything whose depth is enormous or unfathomable.

ANSWER: B. This line originates in the tome *Beyond Good and Evil*. In case it wasn't clear, the other half of the aphorism reads: "Whoever fights with monsters should see to it that he does not become one himself."

"Tell all the truth, but tell it slant."

A Herman Melville

....

B Richard Nixon

....

C Emily Dickinson

....

D Bob Dylan

....

SEE ALSO:

> "We all know that art is not truth. Art is a lie that makes us realize truth."
>
> —PABLO PICASSO

ANSWER: C. Dickinson was known for using deceptively simple language to deliver profound poetic insights. As she concludes in the final lines of this poem: "The Truth must dazzle gradually / Or every man be blind."

"The truth will set you free. But not until it is finished with you."

A David Foster Wallace

B Deepak Chopra

C Michel Foucault

D Gloria Steinem

"There is nothing more boring than the truth."

—CHARLES BUKOWSKI

ANSWER: A. Wallace's absurdist magnum opus *Infinite Jest*, at nearly 1,100 pages, contains numerous quotable adages. This line belongs to Lyle, a mystical yogi-like weight room attendant at a tennis youth academy.

"To be, or not to be, that is the question."

A Hamlet

B Othello

C Macbeth

D Titus Andronicus

FACT-CHECK

Perhaps this was a pressing question in Shakespeare's time, but today, humanity's deepest queries are somewhat different. Some of the most commonly Googled questions include "Why is the sky blue?" and "Is water wet?"

ANSWER: A. The most famous (and most parodied) of all of Shakespeare's soliloquies, Hamlet's "To be or not to be" speech shows the title character contemplating suicide amid his descent into madness.

"A dream you dream alone is only a dream. A dream you dream together is reality."

A Aung San Suu Kyi

B Yoko Ono

C Carl Jung

D Rumi

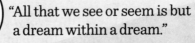

COUNTER POINT "All that we see or seem is but a dream within a dream."

—EDGAR ALLAN POE

ANSWER: B. In his last major interview, published two days before he died, John Lennon touchingly recalled this line—written by Ono decades earlier—in response to a question about their home life.

DIFFICULTY LEVEL

"In the future everybody will be world-famous for fifteen minutes."

A Marshall McLuhan

B Joan Didion

C Andy Warhol

D Aldous Huxley

COUNTER POINT

"In the future everybody will be anonymous for 15 minutes."

—BANKSY (popularized by)

ANSWER: C. The 1960s pop art pioneer made this expression one of his taglines, though later he admitted to growing bored with it. His updated version: "In fifteen minutes everybody will be famous."

"If we must choose between them, it is far safer to be feared than loved."

A Grigori Rasputin

B Sun Tzu

C Catherine the Great

D Niccolò Machiavelli

DID YOU KNOW?

Whatever the truth of this sentiment, fear and love prompt quite different responses in the brain. Fear, for instance, activates the amygdala, which helps us react quickly to danger. In contrast, love deactivates the amygdala. In a sense, love conquers fear.

ANSWER: D. Machiavelli wrote *The Prince* (1513), his influential treatise on gaining and holding power, with an eye toward impressing the Florentine ruler Lorenzo di Piero de Medici, who likely preferred the "fear" option.

"Out of the crooked timber of humanity, no straight thing was ever made."

A Judith Butler

B Martin Luther

C Charlotte Brontë

D Immanuel Kant

DID YOU KNOW?

Each of us is a unique snowflake, and not just because of our fingerprints. Other reliable biometric identifiers—characteristics that can tell individuals apart—include retinal patterns, ear shape, written signature, typing style, and even body odor.

ANSWER: D. The German Enlightenment philosopher used this apt metaphor to illustrate how all-too-fallible humans need a strong leader to rule over them. Otherwise, Kant wrote, "each of them will always abuse his freedom."

"This long course in human wickedness had taught us— the lesson of the fearsome, word-and-thought-defying banality of evil."

A Truman Capote

B Martin Heidegger

C Hannah Arendt

D Susan Sontag

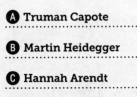

WORD UP

Banal, meaning trite or lacking in originality, originated with an Old French word used to designate communal goods available to serfs, such as community mills. What is banal, then, is what is known to everyone— not just to the nobility.

ANSWER: C. Arendt coined the powerful phrase "banality of evil" in her report on the trial of Nazi Holocaust administrator Adolf Eichmann, who claimed he was only following orders.

"I think, therefore I am."

A Marcus Aurelius

B Gautama Buddha

C René Descartes

D Nicolas Cage

"'I think, therefore I am' is the statement of an intellectual who underrates toothaches."

—MILAN KUNDERA

ANSWER: C. Descartes's famous motto was an attempt to find a logical foundation for the idea that we really do exist. Elsewhere, he explained: "We cannot doubt of our existence while we doubt."

"Life is managed, not cured."

A Hippocrates

·····································

B Florence Nightingale

·····································

C Dr. Phil

·····································

D Jean-Paul Sartre

·····································

SEE ALSO:

"Life is a sexually transmitted disease."

—GRAFFITI FOUND ON
THE LONDON UNDERGROUND

ANSWER: C. This is the seventh of Dr. Phil's Ten Life Laws. The self-help guru's axioms range from the banal—"You either get it, or you don't"—to the profound—"There is no reality, only perception."

"It takes a great deal of bravery to stand up to our enemies, but just as much to stand up to our friends."

A John Kerry

B Beatrix Potter

C Eleanor Roosevelt

D Albus Dumbledore

DID YOU KNOW?

Though people are susceptible to peer pressure at nearly every stage of life, it's between the crucial ages of 14 and 18 that most youth actively develop their ability to say "no" to friends.

ANSWER: D. The wizened Hogwarts headmaster (from the Harry Potter series) has a penchant for dispensing kid-friendly wisdom.

"Art is ugly things that become beautiful; fashion is beautiful things that become ugly."

 A Doris Duke

B Yves Saint Laurent

C Gore Vidal

D Coco Chanel

SEE ALSO:

"The fashion of this world passeth away."

—1 CORINTHIANS

ANSWER: D. The fashion icon left quite a number of quotable maxims—which some believe share at least part authorship with her onetime lover and lifelong friend, poet Pierre Reverdy.

"The mass of men lead lives of quiet desperation."

 A Erich Fromm

B Henry David Thoreau

 C Virginia Woolf

D Jean-Luc Godard

SEE ALSO:

"Hanging on in quiet desperation is the English way."

—ROGER WATERS (Pink Floyd)

ANSWER: B. Evidently, spending two years, two months, and two days alone next to a pond in the middle of nowhere brought Thoreau to conclusions like this, which he recorded in his essential work of transcendentalism, *Walden*.

"In its majestic equality, the law forbids rich and poor alike to sleep under bridges, beg in the streets, and to steal bread."

Ⓐ Thomas Paine

....

Ⓑ Anatole France

....

Ⓒ Upton Sinclair

....

Ⓓ Dorothy Day

....

SEE ALSO:

"Justice is incidental to law and order."

—J. EDGAR HOOVER

ANSWER: B. A giant of French literature, the *fin de siècle* novelist and poet was also a fierce social critic. "Literature is my hobby," France once said. "I should have liked to have been in politics."

DIFFICULTY LEVEL

"You see, but you do not observe."

A Marcel Duchamp

B Confucius

C Sherlock Holmes

D Darth Vader

DID YOU KNOW?

In a famous study, subjects watch a video of two teams passing basketballs and try to count how many passes one team makes. Midway through, a man in a gorilla suit strolls by—a non sequitur that only half of the subjects end up noticing.

ANSWER: C. Arthur Conan Doyle's story "Scandal in Bohemia" tells of a caper involving a retired opera singer, a blackmail intrigue, and an elaborately disguised King of Bohemia. Naturally, Holmes sees through it all.

"I hate to advocate drugs, alcohol, violence, or insanity to anyone, but they've always worked for me."

A Hunter S. Thompson

B Courtney Love

C Charlie Sheen

D William S. Burroughs

SEE ALSO:

"I've never had a problem with drugs. I've had problems with the police."

—KEITH RICHARDS

ANSWER: A. Thompson popularized the "gonzo" style in journalism in the 1970s by inserting himself—and his substance-fueled antics—into the stories he reported.

WISDOM & MISCELLANY

329

"Be less curious about people and more curious about ideas."

 A Ada Lovelace

B Marie Curie

 C Richard Feynman

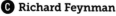 **D** William Safire

> **WORD UP**
>
> Though we now know the word "curious" by its common meaning, describing a desire to learn, nineteenth-century booksellers used the term as a euphemism for pornographic material.

ANSWER: B. As the story goes, Marie gave this answer to an American reporter who mistook her for the maid and asked for some juicy gossip.

DIFFICULTY LEVEL

"In the struggle
between yourself and
the world, side with
the world."

A Franz Kafka

B Terry Gilliam

C Samuel Beckett

D Lily Tomlin

> **SEE ALSO:**
>
> "Life is a gamble,
> at terrible odds—
> if it was a bet you
> wouldn't take it."
>
> —TOM STOPPARD

ANSWER: A. Though Kafka could come off as a bit of a pessimist, his novels and notebooks were often shot through with a dark, absurdist humor. He once wrote to a lover, "I'm even known for my propensity to laugh."

"Man is born free, and everywhere he is in chains."

 A Frederick Douglass

B Martin Luther King Jr.

C Karl Marx

 D Jean-Jacques Rousseau

FACT-CHECK The total number of people who are currently imprisoned is probably around 11 million, or about 0.15 percent.

ANSWER: D. Rousseau begins his book *The Social Contract* with this adage. His ideas went on to play a powerful role in the revolutionary movements that swept Europe in the eighteenth and nineteenth centuries.

"You don't need to go to church to be a Christian. If you go to Taco Bell, that doesn't make you a taco."

Ⓐ Jerry Falwell

Ⓑ Donald Trump

Ⓒ Meryl Streep

Ⓓ Justin Bieber

FACT-CHECK

Thanks to technology, there's some literal truth here. With the advent of live video streaming, thousands of gamers now attend virtual church services without having to leave home.

ANSWER: D. An international pop star at the age of 15, Bieber can be excused for the occasional non sequitur. But that doesn't mean he can't occasionally blurt out profundities. "I wasn't made," he once said, "I was found."

"Tragedy is if I cut my finger . . . Comedy is if you walk into an open sewer and die."

A Sarah Silverman

B Patrick Bateman (*American Psycho*)

C Larry David

D Mel Brooks

DID YOU KNOW?

The notion of *schadenfreude*—mirth at the misfortune of others—has long been fundamental to comedy. That's why some Greek thinkers even saw laughter as a vice. Plato even went so far as to recommend regulating comedy in his *Republic*.

ANSWER: D. Before Brooks made hit movies like *Blazing Saddles* and *The Producers*, he and partner Carl Reiner performed a skit called "The 2,000 Year Old Man," in which he dispensed pearls of loony wisdom like this.

"Every man prays in his own language."

A Duke Ellington

B Bhagwan Shree Rajneesh

C William Penn

D Pope Francis

DID YOU KNOW?

There are an estimated 6,000 to 7,000 languages spoken throughout the world—and the Bible has been translated into at least 2,500 of them.

ANSWER: A. The jazz legend gave this title to one of the songs in his so-called Sacred Concerts, live performances of original works that Ellington described as "the most important thing I have ever done."

"I have a new philosophy—I only dread one day at a time."

A George Carlin

B Charlie Brown

C Wilford Brimley

D Droopy

SEE ALSO:

"Life is far too important a thing ever to talk seriously about it."

—OSCAR WILDE

ANSWER: B. Charlie Brown's pessimism is what made *Peanuts* so relatable. As creator Charles Schulz wrote: "All the loves in the strip are unrequited; all the baseball games are lost; all the test scores are D-minuses; the Great Pumpkin never comes; and the football is always pulled away."

"Don't Gobblefunk around with words."

Ⓐ Spiro Agnew

Ⓑ Roald Dahl

Ⓒ Dr. Seuss

Ⓓ Lewis Carroll

SEE ALSO:

"I consider looseness with words no less of a defect than looseness of the bowels."

—JOHN CALVIN

ANSWER: B. The author of kids' classics like *Matilda* and *Charlie and the Chocolate Factory* had a perfect ear for gibberish. The Oxford English Dictionary includes five novel words and phrases coined by Dahl.

"If God did not exist, it would be necessary to invent him."

Ⓐ Richard Dawkins

···

Ⓑ Cornel West

···

Ⓒ Saint Thomas Aquinas

···

Ⓓ Voltaire

···

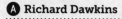

FACT-CHECK Not necessarily. A study of beliefs held by cultures throughout Austronesia—which includes parts of Southeast Asia, Oceania, and East Africa—found that numerous complex societies developed *without* belief in an all-powerful God.

ANSWER: D. Perhaps the most prolific of the Enlightenment thinkers, Voltaire launched numerous broadsides against organized religion and government figures. He was twice imprisoned and for a time exiled in England.

"There are known knowns; there are things we know we know. We also know there are known unknowns; that is to say we know there are some things we do not know. But there are also unknown unknowns—the ones we don't know we don't know."

A Donald Rumsfeld

B Bill Clinton

C Raymond Chandler

D Bertrand Russell

COUNTER POINT

"I know nothing except the fact of my ignorance." —SOCRATES

ANSWER: A. Spoken in the leadup to the Iraq War, this remark would become infamous. But the Secretary of Defense later claimed he was only borrowing from terminology that had been used in intelligence circles for years.

ACKNOWLEDGMENTS

At the outset, I need to thank my first and most important readers: my family. In virtually every writing project I have undertaken, I have known that I could rely on Mom, Dad, Kyle, and Jenny to provide an audience. Their care and encouragement have meant the world to me.

For extending me this opportunity and seeing it through with diligence and good humor, I owe enormous gratitude to my editor and dear friend Danny Cooper. I have been continually impressed with Danny's unerring good judgment—his faith in my own abilities notwithstanding. I know few people, if any, whose sensibilities align so closely with my own.

Finally, I am indebted to my partner Dana for her love and her patience with me and my Quotes. For months on end, night and day, she endured a regular stream of quote-related queries: Which Martha Stewart quote is funnier? Does this sound more like Churchill or FDR? Did you hear what Cézanne said about Monet? When my own judgment failed me, I relied on Dana for her reliably honest opinions and unfailing moral support. Words cannot convey my love for her.